# WELCOME TO BAHRAIN





World Trade Center

NOVOTEL

# Getting to Bahrain

## By air

Gulf Air is the only airline to operate direct flights to Bahrain, from London Heathrow to Manama, which takes around 7 hours. Flights with one stopover also leave from New York JFK, Los Angeles and Sydney. Other airlines operate non-direct flights only.

**Bahrain International Airport** – *Muharraq* - *973 8000 7777* - *www.bahrainairport.bh*. This was the first international airport established in the Arabian Gulf (1927). It served as a stopover on the London to Delhi route and remains a popular hub for travellers en route to Asia. As a sign of its importance, Bahrain welcomed Concorde's first commercial flight, from London, in 1976.

A new state-of-the-art terminal costing 1.1 billion dollars was opened in 2021, raising the airport's capacity to 14 million passengers, with all the technological innovations to go with it. Everything is brand new, spotless and rarely busy, so passing through border control is fast and easy.

**Connection with Manama** – The airport is located in Muharraq, 5 miles from Manama city centre. A taxi ride from the airport to Manama (for example, Bab al Bahrain, Bahrain Bay or Block 338) takes around 10-15 min., depending on traffic.

If you have a stopover in Bahrain for a few hours, it's easy to make the most of it to visit the old town of Muharraq.

**Bus** – Exit 4 in the arrivals hall - bus lines A1, A2, 10 and 11 all pass through Manama Bus Terminal. 300 fils a ticket.

**Taxi** – Opposite gate B. 7-8 BD to get to the city centre.

Bahrain Taxi Group – *6696 6976* - *www.bh-taxigroup.com*.

Arabian Taxi – *1746 1746* - *www.arabiantaxi.bh*.

### Best gateway into the Gulf countries?

Bahrain makes an ideal gateway into the countries of the Gulf region. Thanks to the multitude of flights going there, the country's close proximity by road and air with Saudi Arabia, improving all the time, and flights to neighbouring Kuwait and Qatar, the United Arab Emirates and Oman, Bahrain makes it easy to explore the diversity of history and culture in the Arabian Peninsula. The Kingdom of Bahrain can also be combined with countries further afield, in Asia for example. By flying with Gulf Air, avid travellers can stop a few nights in Bahrain to explore the 'Pearl of the Gulf' before heading on to their final destination.



Statue of a pearl diver in the sculpture courtyard at the Bahrain National Museum.

# Unmissable

**our selection of must-see sites**

★★★ **Pearling Path**
Map E2 - p. 29

★ **Manama Souq**
Map DE2 - p. 14

★ **Bahrain Bay**
Map DE2 - p. 20

★★★ **Qal'at Al Bahrain**
Map D2 - p. 50

e the map of Manama
inside the guide

★★ **Bahrain National Museum**
Map E2 - p. 22

★ **Al Fateh Grand Mosque**
Map E2 - p. 27

★★ **National Charter Monument**
Map D4 - p. 61

★★ **Manamat Al Gosaibi**
Map DE2 - p. 18

# Our top picks

**Tuck into a traditional breakfast at Haji's Cafe in Manama.** On the menu, an assortment of plates of vegetables, beans, cheese... served with piping hot, freshly baked bread. Plus get to rub shoulders with the locals. *p. 70.*

**Dig into 4,000 years of history at Qal'at Al Bahrain**. Nestled in an ancient harbour, this site looks its best at sunset. Use your imagination to picture ships sailing into port from India, and climb up to the Portuguese fort's walkway to take in views of the entire magnificent complex. *p. 50.*



**Glimpse into the life of an emir in the palace of Sheikh Isa bin Ali Al Khalifa in the heart of Muharraq**. Happily lose yourself in a maze of buildings and courtyards, and admire the finely crafted decorative features on the terraces. It's also the ideal opportunity to find out just how efficient those famous wind towers are. *p. 43.*

**Attend the Bahrain Formula One Grand Prix,** the island's hottest ticket, if you time your trip right. A buzzing atmosphere and unbelievable experience, even if motorsports aren't your thing. And contrary to expectation, it attracts a young, international crowd, so your teenage kids will love it. *p. 62.*

**Test your racing mettle on Sakhir's International Karting Circuit**. Pilot high-performance vehicles on a world-class track with a huge board at the starting line displaying your lap time... and your photo! *p. 64.*

**Be transported by sut, traditional Bahraini folk music**, in the Mohammed bin Faris concert hall. It's every Thursday evening, and it's free. You can also catch folk music performed every Saturday evening outside the Post Office Museum at Bab Al Bahrain. *p. 35.*

**Venture out to the Tree of Life,** said to be the last vestige of the Garden of Eden, and ponder a mystery: how does life thrive in the middle of the desert? *p. 64.*

**Contemplate contemporary art at the RAK Foundation** and tune into the beauty and serenity of this intimate art gallery. *p. 59.*

**Watch the sunset while sipping a cocktail on a rooftop in Block 338, in Adliya**, Manama's hippest neighbourhood. And if you like the vibe, stay and dance to the beats of the DJs who set the Bahraini party crowd on fire. *p. 88.*

**Make like a pearl diver** in the turquoise waters of the Arabian Gulf. All you need is a snorkel and mask, and there's a 90% chance of finding a pearl

©Eric Sander (ericsander.com)

International Karting Circuit.

or two. Well, that's what the tourist information office says! p. 100.

**Savour a cardamom coffee at Bu Khalaf Coffee Shop**, in business since the 1930s. It's been updated since, however, with gorgeous traditional furniture and shabby-chic decor. p. 79.

**Swim in the crystal-clear waters lapping Al Jaradah Island**, in the middle of the sea. The must-do? Organise a picnic with the boat hire firm and feast on a barbecue, Robinson Crusoe style. p. 66.

**Dive 8 metres down to hunt for oysters**, navigate a merchant ship from India to Arabia... virtually, of course, all possible thanks to the amazing immersive installations at the National Charter Monument. p. 62.

**Appreciate the ancestral skills of shipbuilders** constructing *dhows*, the traditional boats used in the Arabian Gulf. They work from memory, reproducing the teachings of their master. p. 44.

# Bahrain in 3 days

## Day 1

**Morning**

Before you do anything else, head to **Haji's Cafe** *(p. 70)* for the full Bahraini breakfast experience. Then dive into **Manama Souq★** *(p. 14)* and get lost in its maze of glittering jewellery, craft and carpet shops and stalls brimming with spices. Along the way, you'll come across mosques, a church, a Hindu temple and a synagogue, a microcosm of the island's diversity. Not to mention **Manamat Al Gosaibi★★** *(p. 18)*, a supremely renovated traditional house.



**Midday**

Lunch at **Indigo Terrace** *(p. 70)*.

**Afternoon**

Visit the **Bahrain National Museum★★** *(p. 22)* for a staggering exploration of over 4,000 years of history, brilliantly brought to life. The recreation of a traditional souq on the upper level is fascinating. Enjoy a break in the museum café, soaking up views of the bay before swinging by the **National Theatre★** *(p. 26)* next door.

**Evening**

Head to **Bahrain Bay★** *(p. 20)* for dinner at the **Fish Market**, which is actually a restaurant, and a first-rate one at that *(p. 71)*. Try and score a table on the terrace with bay views if it's not too hot.

## Day 2

**Morning**

Explore **Muharraq★★★** *(p. 29)*, Manama's twin city. Its history is entwined with that of sailors and pearl fishers. The waymarked **Pearling Path★★★** *(p. 34)* takes you on a tour of lovingly restored period buildings, opulent villas, and humble fishermen's dwellings.

**Midday**

Have lunch at **Dona's Wonders** *(p. 74)*.

**Afternoon**

Visit **Qal'at Al Bahrain★★★** *(p. 50)*, the epicentre of ancient Dilmun where 4,000 years ago ships from India, East Africa and Mesopotamia dropped anchor. Then, when the afternoon light is at its most radiant, explore the **Portuguese fort** *(p. 53)* which towers over the site. The museum's café terrace is a lovely spot to watch the sunset.

### More time on your hands?

After three busy days of seeing the main sights, there is plenty more for you to enjoy during your stay. Treat yourself to a trip out to **Al Jaradah Island** *(p. 66)*, get an adrenaline fix at the **International Karting Circuit in Sakhir** *(p. 64)*, discover the traditional **potters in A'ali** *(p. 56)* or the Royal Mounds in Dilmun, soak up some rays on **Al Jazair beach** (or your resort's private beach), try out the amazing food choices around Manama, shop till you drop in the malls... the possibilities are endless.

©Eric Sander (ericsander.com)

Take a cruise and dive for pearls at Al Jaradah Island.



### Evening

Venture into **Block 338**, Manama's party central *(p. 27)*. Dine at **Clay** *(p. 72)* for Asian-Peruvian fusion food, or **Gunaydin** *(p. 72)* for amazing Turkish cuisine. Then wet your whistle at **Iris** *(p. 88)*, one of the hippest rooftops in town.

## Day 3

Spend a day exploring the south of the island.

### Morning

Start at **Al Khamis★★** *(p. 28)*, Bahrain's oldest mosque, then take the road to **Riffa** *(p. 58)*: visit the fort, from where you can see sweeping vistas of the centre of the island, then the **RAK Foundation★★** *(p. 59)*, an astonishing collection of contemporary art (make sure you book).

### Midday

Lunch at **My Cafe** *(p. 77)*.

### Afternoon

Experience the **National Charter Monument★★** *(p. 61)*: its museum immerses you fully in the island's history and traditions. Mind-blowing! Venture further south to witness the **Tree of life★**, Bahrain's best-known symbol *(p. 64)*.

### Evening

Enjoy a meal at **Villa Mamas** *(p. 74)* in **Saar** before returning to Manama.

# VISIT BAHRAIN

The sculpture courtyard at the Bahrain National Museum.

# Bahrain today

The smallest sovereign Arab country (293.4 sq. mi) is constantly expanding. Every year, it encroaches nearly a square mile more into the sea to build soaring skyscrapers and state-of-the-art buildings. So is Bahrain in the throes of rapid globalisation? Yes and no. The kingdom is vigorously cultivating its authenticity while, in the shadows of glittering glass towers, you can witness fishermen heading out to sea, get lost in labyrinthine souqs or venture out to the countryside to meet farmers tending their crops. But there's a definite upside to modernisation: an incredible offering of high-end hotels, a multitude of fine-dining venues flying the flag of every world cuisine and first-rate amenities and facilities.



## A tradition of welcoming others

Bahrain means 'two seas' in Arabic, referring to the island's freshwater springs and the salty waters of the Arabian Gulf. They even say that it is this particular aquatic blend that lends Bahrain's famous pearls their lustre. A strategic port of call along maritime routes for over 4,000 years, the island has welcomed sailors and merchants from all around onto its shores. No wonder then that the country has such strong traditions of hosting and hospitality. Today still, the entire world is made welcome in Bahrain. Out of the 1.5 million inhabitants in the kingdom, less than half are Bahraini born and bred. Most of the population hail from India, the Philippines, Bangladesh and other Arab nations, creating a rich mix of cultures and languages. Manama's souq might well be described as 'Little India': almost all of the stalls are run by shopkeepers originating from the Indian subcontinent, and the enticing aromas of curry emanate from the market's abundant food counters and street vendors. There's even a 200-year-old Hindu temple built within its maze of alleys.

## An outward-looking kingdom

Today, this dynamic dwarf state is leaping onto the regional and international stage, for example by establishing full diplomatic relations with Israel in 2020 and hosting a visit by Pope Francis in 2022. Sport is another area where Bahrain is fostering its international image. Under the stewardship of Prince Salman bin Hamad Al Khalifa, the Kingdom of Bahrain was the first Arab country to host the Formula One Grand Prix following the opening of the Bahrain International Circuit in Sakhir in 2004. Since 2017, a Bahraini pro cycling team has participated every year in the Tour de France. Bahrain's sovereign wealth fund acquired a 20% stake in Paris FC in 2020. And in 2022, Bahrain was in talks to buy Milan AC, a deal that ultimately didn't go ahead.

## And what about oil?

A pioneer of the region's oil-drilling industry, in recent years Bahrain has been actively pursuing a post-oil future. Even if the country gets revenue from two oil fields, its production is disproportionate to that of its neighbours in the Gulf, with oil and gas barely accounting for 10% of GDP. By far its biggest industrial sectors are aluminium – the country being home to Aluminium Bahrain (ALBA), the world's second-largest smelter after China –, banking and finance and, of course, tourism.

## Twelve million annual visitors...

...four-fifths of whom are Saudis: at the weekend, endless lines of traffic crossing the bridge connecting the two countries, the King Fahd Causeway, make for a familiar sight.

While the 'Pearl of the Gulf' is still far from being swarmed by Western tourists, things are changing, as the kingdom has so many reasons to visit. Much like its neighbours, Bahrain has its fair share of dizzying skyscrapers, but it has also firmly held on to its historic areas like Manama's souq and Muharraq Old City, which the authorities are restoring to its former glory. This is the heart and soul of Bahrain that is being preserved in the shape of its monuments, such as the Pearling Path, listed as a UNESCO World Heritage site in 2012.

## The place of women

Women occupy a visible and often eminent place in Bahraini society, as ministers, CEOs, star chefs and taxi drivers. It's a tradition that goes far back. The first girls' school in the region was opened here, in 1932. Some even say that the legacy can be traced back to the pearl economy. When the men left for sea, the women were left in charge. The town of sea folk, Muharraq, became the city of women. Some women even led prayer.

## Why visit Bahrain?

In the same day, you can visit a 4,000-year-old archaeological site, be blown away by the cutting-edge developments in Bahrain Bay, Manama's latest hospitality hub studded with jaw-dropping feats of architecture, then round off the day sipping a sundowner on a rooftop bar in Block 338, Manama's hotspot neighbourhood. Not to mention swimming, taking a sea excursion for a diving expedition in translucent waters in the hope of discovering an oyster harbouring a pearl, exploring art galleries, shopping in luxury malls or designer boutiques – experiences which make Bahrain a destination in its own right where you can spend a week without ever getting bored.

Bahrain's flag: the five white triangle points symbolise the five pillars of Islam.

# Manama ★

**The capital makes for an enticing introduction to the kingdom. Futuristic is the first word that springs to mind, its land reclaimed from the sea the foundation for architects the world over to come and build sublime and surprising mega structures. Yet it has not abandoned its past either, as it strives to preserve both its traditional souq and the memory of the country's long history in its fascinating National Museum. Not to mention that Manama knows how to lay on a good time, with a tantalising array of restaurants and the hip Block 338 district.**

▶ **Getting there:** the international airport is 5 miles north of the city.

**Area map pp. 16, 24-25 Detachable map DE2.**

▶ **Tip:** wherever you choose to stay, in Bahrain Bay reflecting modern-day Manama or closer to the Old City, there's no better way to feel the pulse of the place than starting your tour with Manama Souq. Fuel up on a traditional breakfast at **Haji's Cafe** (*p. 70*), a local institution.

*Our addresses pp. 70, 78, 82, 86 and 90.*



## MANAMA SOUQ★

**EF1** *Plan for 4 hours of walking.*
Immerse yourself in Manama's historic centre with, star of the show, the Gold Souq; a jumble of period houses, many beautifully restored; the constant waft of aromatic spices in the air, and the bustling throng of Indian stallholders who own the lion's share of the businesses in this vibrant market.

## Bab Al Bahrain★

**E1** Dating from 1945, this monumental gateway was built during the British occupation. It was even once the office of the colonial administrators. Back then, the structure stood at the water's edge. Land reclamation has meant that the sea has now been pushed back by over half a mile.

## Post Office Museum★

**E1** *Daily ex. Fri 9am-5pm.*
Set within the protectorate capital's former post office, this bijou museum provides an entertaining retrospective of the history of Bahrain through postage stamps. Philatelists will appreciate too the stamps on display from around the world. On the upper level, a tiny café makes an ideal spot to watch the bustle below (*p. 78*). Catch live folk music outside the museum every Saturday, from 7pm.

## The Mall

**E1** An extension of the Bab Al Bahrain, this handsome modern building is reminiscent of a traditional caravanserai. Under one roof, you'll find fab traditional craft shops, cafés

Manama Souq, a riot of colours and aromas.

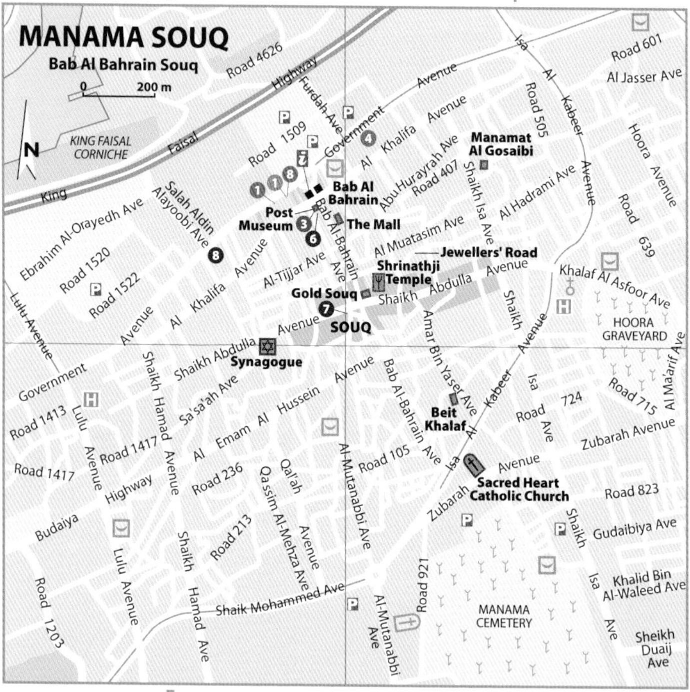


**WHERE TO EAT**

Haji's Café .................. 1

Indigo Terrace .............. 8

**WHERE TO DRINK**

The Dot Coffee ............ 3

**SHOPPING**

Made in Bahrain Gift Shop .. 6

Kingdom of Perfumes ...... 7

Gold City .................. 8

**NIGHTLIFE**

Alto ....................... 4

**WHERE TO STAY**

The Merchant House ....... 1

and restaurants, including **Naseef**, a Bahraini institution (*Addresses p. 74*). Make your way up to the mezzanine level to peruse the carpets and rugs.

## The Gold Souq

**F1** The Mall's main street and side alleys are lined with dozens of jewellery shops, their windows gleaming with gold, rings, pendants and other treasures, often attracting crowds of figures dressed head to toe in black, the typical garb of Saudi women whose visit to Bahrain is usually a pretext for a shopping trip. Further along on the left is the entrance to the Gold Souq, looking like some kind of Fort Knox behind reinforced doors providing extra security for the most renowned jewellers. Save this for now as you'll come back through this way later if you follow our itinerary. For the time being, after The Mall take any of the turnings on your right to enter the warren of passageways that form the souq. Al Hadrami Avenue, for example, which is an avenue in name only.

## Inside the souq

There's barely enough room to pass between the stalls on both sides peddling everything from consumer goods and fabrics from India and elsewhere to enticing pastries and spices (cinnamon, cardamom, cumin, turmeric, saffron and *bezar*, a traditional spice blend), the aromas luring you deeper into the market. Browse at your leisure before turning down any of the alleys running on the right towards Sheikh Abdullah Ave., which is more an avenue in the traditional sense.

## Synagogue

**E1-2** *Shaikh Abdulla Ave. - daily ex. Sat 9am-5pm.*
Settling from at least as far back as the mid-19th century, Bahrain's Jewish community was 850 strong in 1940. After the State of Israel was created, only a handful of Jews chose to stay in Bahrain, compelled to practise their faith at home following the closure of the only synagogue. The Abraham Accords (2020), establishing full diplomatic relations between the Kingdom of Bahrain and Israel, prompted the restoration and reopening of the synagogue. Shabbat is observed every Saturday among the 50 or so Jews who call Bahrain home today. A fascinating film *(in English)* tells the history of the Jewish community and the synagogue.
*Follow the road to Bab Al Bahrain Ave. On the corner is the Gold Souq (see opposite). Turn left then take the first road on the right.*

## Shrinathji Temple

**F1** *Daily 6am-7pm.*
At the end of a narrow alley where worshippers can stop to buy flowers and incense as offerings to their deities, Manama's Hindu temple has stood in the centre of a large courtyard for over 200 years, from when the first Indian migrant workers arrived on the island. Followers of Shiva or Vishnu, Manama's Hindus devoutly attend the temple for the daily *darshans*, rituals when prayers are chanted in honour

of the gods (*at 6am, 7:30am, 11am and 5:15pm*). One of the temple custodians will happily take you on a tour of the building.
*Continue straight along Shaikh Isa Ave. before turning left then taking the third alley on the right.*

## Manamat Al Gosaibi★★

**F1** *Lane 521 - daily ex. Fri 8am-2pm, 4pm-7pm - paid entry with the Culture Pass only, on sale here and at the Shaikh Ebrahim Center (**p. 103**).*
This is the perfect example of the kind of restoration we love to see in Bahrain: the rewarding blend of traditional architecture and contemporary art. On one side you have the meticulously restored family home, on the other a modern extension that houses a lovely café (which serves only coffee). Separating the two is a stunning bamboo garden designed by Madison Cox, the celebrated landscaper to the rich and famous and director of the Majorelle Gardens in Marrakesh. The various rooms are dedicated to the memory of Ghazi Al Gosaibi (1940-2010), one of the most widely respected contemporary Arabic authors. While he was born and died in Saudi Arabia, he spent his childhood in this district of Manama. One point of interest above the patio is an installation by Nasser Al Salem (born in 1984), a hanging work of art whose curved form celebrates Arabic calligraphy, the Saudi sculptor's primary source of inspiration.

## Jewellers' Road

If you follow Shaikh Isa Avenue towards the sea, some 20 or so boutiques are shielded behind powerful armoured doors. They house Bahrain's most prominent jewellery workshops. They're not completely out of bounds to visitors: ring the bell and try your luck to discover the wealth of treasures inside. We recommend Cádiz Jewellery store, whose pieces are a sublime fusion of traditional forms and contemporary design *(www.cadizjewellery.com)*.
*Retrace your footsteps and walk along Shaikh Isa Ave. for about 600 m before turning right on to Lane 101.*

## Beit Khalaf★

**F2** *Lane 109 - daily ex. Fri 8am-2pm, 4pm-7pm - paid entry: Culture Pass.*
To reach your next destination, you'll pass through a pleasant residential neighbourhood, fringed here and there with various old houses which have seen better days. Dating from the early 1900s, Bait Khalaf was once home to a pearl merchant family. The period building has been beautifully restored and stands as a tribute to how its former occupants lived back in the day. Note the stunning decorative engravings on the ground floor. In several rooms on the upper floor you can imagine how the former occupants would have lived and worked, with displays of antique equipment used to weigh and grade the pearls they caught. The wood panelling surrounding the balconies is remarkably intricate. From the terrace, visitors can take in views of the neighbouring rooftops and the skyline of the new city. The fine-looking

©Eric Sander (ericsander.com)

The Gold Souq, a real Ali Baba's cave.



residence opposite Khalaf House, also exquisitely restored, still belongs to the Khalaf family.

*Turn left as you exit the building and follow the street round to the left.*

## Sacred Heart Catholic Church

**F2** *329 Isa Al Kabeer Ave. - ✆ 1725 3598 - www.sacredheartchurchbahrain.org - daily ex. Mon 6am-noon, 3pm-8:45pm.*

Mosques, a synagogue, a Hindu temple and here a Catholic church: the world's major faiths coexist happily in old Manama. Consecrated in 1939, it's the oldest church in the region from the modern period. Since then, the complex has expanded to cater to the growing Catholic community who have arrived from the Philippines, India and elsewhere to work in Bahrain.

The church today is surrounded by various large buildings housing meeting places for the parish, a school and a Carmelite convent. Pope Francis paid an official visit to the Sacred Heart Church during his Bahrain visit in November 2022.

*If you still have the energy, continue on the itinerary to see the last traditional house in the district. From the Sacred Heart Church, take Isa Al Kabeer Ave., turn right at the corner of the American Mission (yet another bell tower on the Manama skyline), follow the cemetery then turn left. The walk to the next site takes around 15 min.*

## Al Arrayed House

**C2** *Palace Rd - daily ex. Fri. 9am-2pm, 4pm-7pm - paid entry: Culture Pass.* Also called the House of Poetry, this beautiful residence constructed in the mid-20th c. was the home of noted Bahraini poet and statesman, Ibrahim Al Arrayed (1908-2002). A selection of personal effects and documents recount the life of the Bombay-born intellectual. The auditorium regularly hosts poetry recitals.

## BAHRAIN BAY★

**C1** Arguably the capital's most scenic place to go for a stroll, where in a single glance you can take in Manama's most iconic modern buildings. This development built entirely on artificially reclaimed land from the sea is set around a lagoon and bisected by a canal lined with places to eat and drink. The Venice of Bahrain if you will. You can even ride in a gondola! Spanning the waterfront opposite is **The Avenues**, one of the city's swankiest shopping destinations (*Addresses p. 83*). The bay gets lively from late afternoon and gradually more animated into the evening. It's the ideal spot to enjoy a night out, especially as some of the capital's finest restaurants are located there (*Addresses p. 70*). A brief survey of Manama's top architectural wonders.



### World Trade Center★

**C2** One of Bahrain's most iconic structures, this 240-metre twin-tower complex is linked by three skybridges each supporting a huge wind turbine. The state-of-the-art building is a master class in design and sustainability from Shaun Killa, the architect behind the mind-blowing Museum of the Future in Dubai. The towers house a Sheraton Hotel, serviced offices and the high-style **Moda Mall** (*Addresses p. 83*). At night, the stunningly illuminated towers are a magical sight!

### United Tower

**C1** It's also known as the Twisted Tower because of its bold spiral design. The 190-metre, 48-storey structure is taken up by offices and the **Wyndham Grand Manama** hotel (*Addresses p. 90*).

### Four Seasons Hotel

**C1** Ensconced on its own artificial island in the centre of Bahrain Bay, at 270 metres and 68 storeys it's the tallest building in Manama (*Addresses p. 91*). Not to mention one of the most audacious architecturally, with its two towers connected by a stack of floors seemingly suspended in mid-air. It was designed by SOM (Skidmore, Owings and Merrill), the American architecture firm that also brought us the Burj Khalifa in Dubai, the world's tallest building (828m).

### Arcapita Mosque

**C1** Towering over the bay, this cube-form mosque, supremely elegant in its simplicity, is another design from the firm SOM. Built out of local stone, it features 50 windows that cast indirect light, keeping the interior relatively cool.

Bahrain Bay, the ultramodern district that bursts into life at night, ideal for getting a feel for the

## DIPLOMATIC AREA

### Bahrain National Museum★★

**C2** *Shaikh Hamad Causeway - ✆ 1729 8178 - daily ex. Tue 8am-8pm - entry 1.1 BD - lovely tea room for a short rest.*

This striking architectural complex on the waterfront features a leafy patio, a sculpture garden, whose pieces include the figure of a pearl fisher, and the museum itself: four white cubic gallery blocks with no apertures, designed to protect the artworks from the scorching sunlight. The museum, designed by Danish architect Knud Holscher, was inaugurated in 1988. The wonderfully presented collections offer an interesting overview of the island's 4,000-plus years of history.

**Hall of Dilmun★★★**. From the mid-3rd millennium BC, the island became an important stop along the main maritime routes connecting India and Mesopotamia. Sumerian texts named this region Dilmun. Archaeological digs since the 1950s show how globalisation was already at play thousands of years ago. The star attraction in the room is the **bull's head made of copper★** (ca. 2500 BC), discovered under Barbar Temple (*p. 53*). This decorative piece would have been attached to a wooden lyre whose model is on display in the Sumerian section. The copper itself came from present-day Oman: the metal was one of the main cargoes transported to the Euphrates. Worth seeing: the collections of Dilmun seals unearthed along the trade routes, between the Euphrates and the Indus Valley.

**Dilmun burial mounds**. They are one of the most spectacular - not to say unique in the world due to their number - characteristics of the Dilmun civilisation (*p. 110*). Archaeologists have discovered almost 12,000 mounds over 21 sites in the western part of the island. Tombs of wealthy dignitaries or members of the ruling family from A'ali (*p. 56*), they have given up significant quantities of objects buried with the bodies, including semi-precious gems and pottery from Persia or Oman. A selection of these artefacts is on display here alongside the meticulous reconstruction of a grave.

Continue to the first floor and the **Hall of Tylos**. After the conquest of Persia by Alexander the Great (323 BC), Dilmun was thrust into the trading system used across the Hellenistic and then Roman worlds. Henceforth known as Tylos, the island remained a prosperous commercial hub between India and the Euphrates. Pearls from the region were exported to Rome. The majority of the objects on show here were unearthed from graves: tombstones marking plots where the deceased were buried upright, one hand raised in salutation to the gods, based on models from Iran, alongside opulent funerary relics including thin strips of gold used to cover the eyes and mouth of the deceased.

**Hall of traditional trades and crafts**. Your visit concludes with the mesmerising reconstruction of a traditional souq with its stalls and workshops. One section is devoted to the pearl, from the activity of pearling through to its place in international trade.

Copper bull's head from the Dilmun civilisation discovered beneath the Barbar Temple.

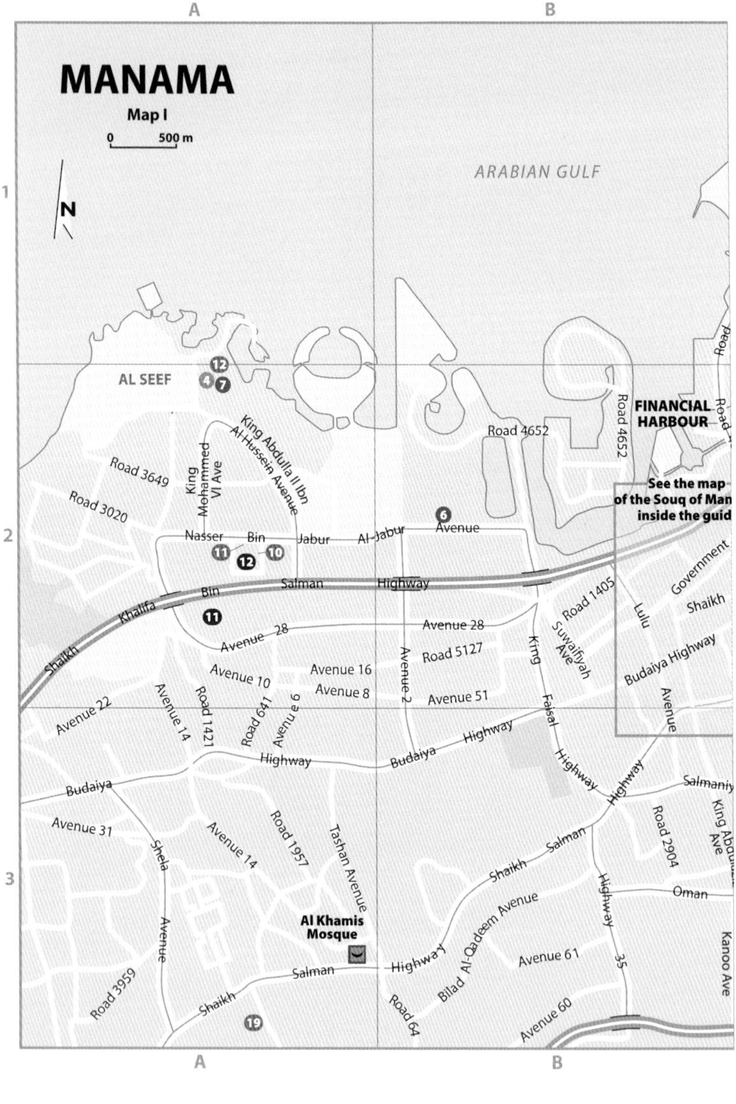

MANAMA
Map I
0
500 m
N
A
B
1
2
3
ARABIAN GULF
AL SEEF
FINANCIAL HARBOUR
See the map of the Souq of Man
inside the guid
Road 3649
Road 3020
King Mohammed VI Ave
King Abdulla II Ibn Al Hussein Avenue
Nasser Bin Jabur
Al-Jabur Avenue
Road 4652
Road 4652
Shaikh Khalifa Bin Salman Highway
Avenue 28
Avenue 28
Road 5127
Avenue 16
Avenue 10
Avenue 8
Avenue 2
Avenue 51
Avenue 22
Avenue 14
Road 1421
Road 641
Avenue 6
Budaiya Highway
Budaiya Highway
King Faisal Highway
Road 1405
Suwaifiyah Ave
Lulu
Government
Shaikh
Budaiya Highway
Avenue
Highway
Salmaniy
Road 2904
King Abd Ave
Avenue 31
Shela Avenue
Avenue 14
Road 1957
Tashan Avenue
Al Khamis Mosque
Shaikh Salman Highway
Shaikh Salman Highway
Bilad Al-Qadeem Avenue
Highway 35
Oman
Avenue 61
Kanoo Ave
Road 3959
Road 64
Avenue 60
Road
Road
12
4
7
6
11
12
10
11
19

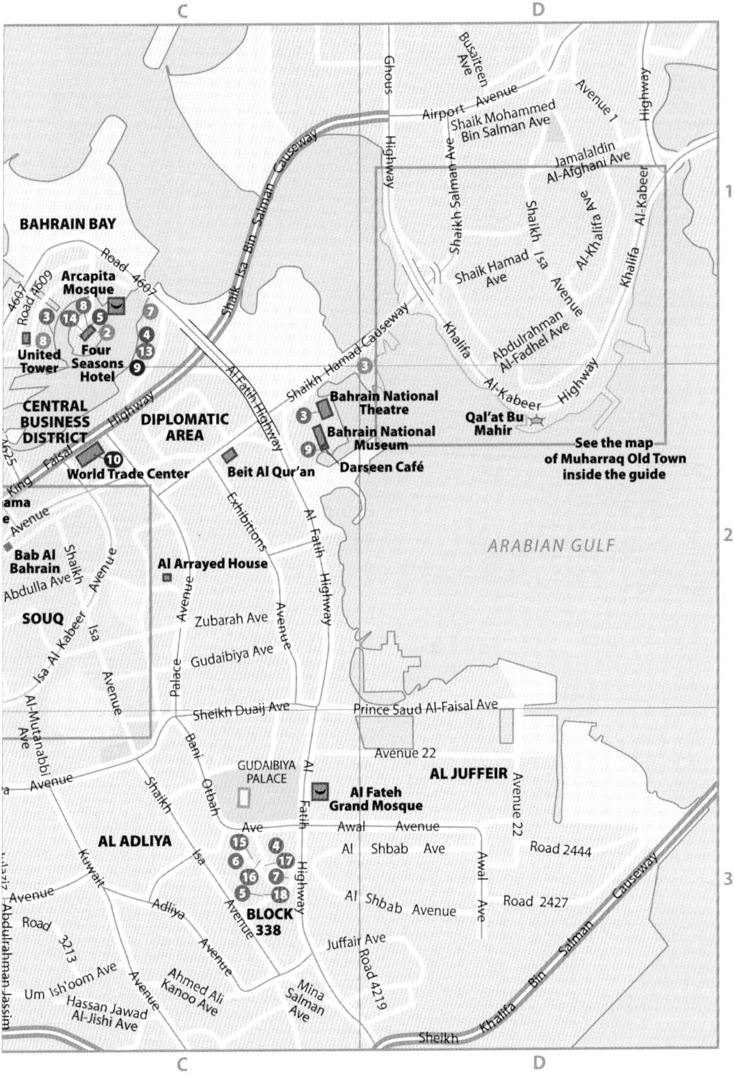

C
D
BAHRAIN BAY
Arcapita Mosque
United Tower
Four Seasons Hotel
CENTRAL BUSINESS DISTRICT
DIPLOMATIC AREA
World Trade Center
Beit Al Qur'an
Bahrain National Theatre
Bahrain National Museum
Darseen Café
Qal'at Bu Mahir
See the map of Muharraq Old Town inside the guide
ARABIAN GULF
Bab Al Bahrain
SOUQ
Al Arrayed House
GUDAIBIYA PALACE
Al Fateh Grand Mosque
AL JUFFEIR
AL ADLIYA
BLOCK 338
Airport Avenue
Shaik Mohammed Bin Salman Ave
Jamalaldin Al-Afghani Ave
Shaik Hamad Ave
Abdulrahman Al-Fadhel Ave
Shaik Isa Bin Salman Causeway
Shaikh Hamad Causeway
Al Fatih Highway
Exhibitions Avenue
Zubarah Ave
Gudaibiya Ave
Palace Avenue
Sheikh Duaij Ave
Prince Saud Al-Faisal Ave
Avenue 22
Bani Otbah Ave
Awal Avenue
Al Shbab Ave
Al Shbab Avenue
Road 2444
Road 2427
Juffair Ave
Road 4219
Mina Salman Ave
Sheikh Khalifa Bin Salman Causeway
Kuwait Avenue
Adliya Avenue
Shaikh Isa Avenue
Ahmed Ali Kanoo Ave
Um Ish'oom Ave
Hassan Jawad Al-Jishi Ave
Road 3213
Abdulrahman Jassim
Al-Mutanabbi Ave
Shaikh Abdulla Ave
Isa Al Kabeer
King Faisal Highway
Road 4609
Road 4607
Ghous Highway
Busaiteen Ave
Avenue 1
Highway
Shaikh Salman Ave
Shaikh Isa Avenue
Al-Khalifa Ave
Al-Kabeer Khalifa Highway
1
2
3

**WHERE TO EAT**
Fish Market Restaurant ..... 3
Fusions by Tala ..... 4
Darseen Cafe ..... 9
Pickl ..... 10
Baker & Spice ..... 11
Cantina Kahlo ..... 12
Lumee ..... 13
CUT by Wolfgang Puck ..... 14
Gunaydin ..... 15
Clay ..... 16
L'Orto ..... 17
Mahonia ..... 18
Tabreez Restaurant ..... 19

**WHERE TO DRINK**
The Orangery ..... 4
Bay View Lounge ..... 5
La Reine Cafe ..... 6
Burlington Club ..... 7

**SHOPPING**
The Avenues Mall ..... 9
Moda Mall ..... 10
The Bahrain Mall ..... 11
Al 'Aali Mall ..... 12

**NIGHTLIFE**
Bahrain National Theater ..... 3
Iris ..... 5
Halo Lounge ..... 6
Gallery 21 ..... 7
Blue Moon Lounge by Wolfgang Puck ..... 8

**WHERE TO STAY**
Four Seasons Hotel Bahrain Bay ..... 2
Novotel Al Dana Resort and Spa ..... 3
Ritz-Carlton Bahrain ..... 4
Hilton Garden Inn ..... 7
Wyndham Grand Manama ..... 8

## Bahrain National Theatre★

**C2** *Shaikh Hamad Causeway - culture.gov.bh/en/authority/cultural_sites/BahrainNationalTheatre - free tours daily ex. Fri 8am-2pm.*



You'd be hard pressed to find a more striking building as this one, which seems to float on the lagoon. Completed in 2012, Bahrain National Theatre was designed by French firm Architecture-Studio, the architects who also conceived the Arab World Institute in Paris, in collaboration with the architect Jean Nouvel. The foyer surrounded by floor-to-ceiling windows is crowned with an aluminium canopy designed to mimic traditional awnings woven from palm leaves. The building interior is well worth a visit: the main auditorium (1,001 seats) is entirely clad in elm, a wood known for its superior acoustic qualities, its undulating surface recalling the hulls of traditional pearling vessels. On the upper level, the foyer is an architectural tour de force graced with white concrete curves. Flanking the exterior, geiger trees with their bright orange flowers bring a splash of greenery and colour to the sleek structure.

## Beit Al Qur'an★

**C2** *Rd 1901, Al Hoora - daily ex. Fri 8:30am-4pm (Sat 1:30pm).*

The 'House of the Quran' harbours a collection of handwritten and printed editions of Islam's holy book. A precious parchment from the 8th c. written in elegant Kufic script is one of the oldest known examples of the Quran. The medieval manuscripts – from Persia, Mesopotamia and North Africa – on display let visitors appreciate the different forms of Arabic writing, illustrating the infinite range of its calligraphic styles. Other artefacts to discover include the earliest printed Quran from Hamburg, Germany, in 1694, as well as translated versions in Latin (1543), Russian, French and other languages, dating from the 16th and 17th centuries.

## JUFFAIR, ADLIYA AND THE SOUTH

### Al Fateh Grand Mosque★

**C3** *Awal Ave. - ✆ 1772 7773 - www.alfatehbh.net - open daily ex. Fri 9am-4pm; tours given by centre guides only, enquire at the reception desk. Men must have arms and legs covered, women are required to wear an* abayah, *provided at reception.*
No expense was spared for the construction of the mosque dedicated to Ahmed Al Fateh, the 'Conqueror' (1725-1795), founder of the Al Khalifa dynasty. The ubiquitous marble was sourced from Carrara, the monumental doors were crafted from Indian teak, the chandelier is made of Swarovski crystal while the lamps are covered in hand-blown glass from Biot (France). Then there's the immense dome over the courtyard which is made entirely of fibreglass. Weighing in at 60 tonnes, it's the largest structure of its type in the world. Make sure you save time to admire the views of the stunning interior spaces from the upper level.

### Block 338

**C3** This district is best explored at night. In a city where air-conditioned cars are the usual (and welcome) mode of transport, it's a delight to mosey around this maze of narrow

©Eric Sander (ericsander.com)

The prayer hall at the Al Fateh Grand Mosque and its staggering Swarovski crystal chandelier.

lanes with its endless rows of bars and restaurants (*Addresses pp. 72 and 88*). On weekend evenings, it's thronged by locals and tourists. Until the early 2000s, Block 338 was a modest residential area which has slowly been taken over by hip venues. The low-rise buildings and the alleys that lend this area its individual look and feel are the last remnants of its former self. Here you can come for a pleasant stroll around its boutiques and art galleries. Take, for instance, the **Al Bareh Art Gallery** , which puts on some of the most avant-garde art shows in the city (*Rd 3601, 38 - www. albareh.com - daily ex. Friday*).

## Al Khamis Mosque★★

**A3** *Shaikh Salman Hwy - 3.5 miles south of the city centre - A1 bus route from Bab Al Bahrain (every 15 min.) - daily ex. Mon 9am-5pm.*

These ruins are said to belong to the earliest mosque in Bahrain. Local tradition has it that it harks back to the 8th c.; archaeologists are less convinced, dating the site to the 12th-13th c. Its twin 21-metre round towers bookend a prayer hall with a flat roof supported by wooden columns. Several digs have unearthed enthralling information about its history. The mosque was apparently once at the centre of a relatively large town. In front of the building, a trench left open by the archaeologists reveals

Al Khamis Mosque, one of the oldest in the Gulf region.

the basin used for performing ritual ablutions. An alley with rows of stalls was excavated, signifying the presence of a souq. They even discovered a *tannur*, a type of clay oven still used nowadays for baking bread. A small-scale museum recounts the history of the digs and presents models and a selection of the relics unearthed. Behind the mosque's visitors centre is a little garden designed by the famous American landscape architect Madison Cox.

# Muharraq ★★★

**Muharraq, or Manama's antithesis. No skyscrapers here, instead a warren of narrow lanes and alleys forming a pleasant residential district. This historic city serves as a formidable custodian of the island's past. The one-time pearling capital has preserved much of its exceptional heritage, including humble pearl divers' houses, opulent villas and warehouses owned by pearl merchants, and royal palaces in the north of the city. Over the past 20 years or so, a dynamic restoration campaign has returned Muharraq to its former glory, culminating in 2012 with it becoming a Unesco World Heritage Site. This restoration has not held back from embracing the bold forms of modern architecture. Ideally, you should factor in a day's walking to explore the main points of interest, setting time aside to browse the souq, stock up on spices or confectionery and take a moment to share a coffee or cake that you are sure to be offered here and there along the way. Because in Muharraq, hospitality is a tradition.**

▶ **Getting there:** take the number 12 bus from Manama Bus Terminal to Qal'at Bu Mahir.

**Area maps pp. 30, 40, 46-47. Detachable map EF1-2.**

▶ **Tip:** some places of interest are closed between 2pm and 4pm so plan a late lunch in one of the excellent local restaurants. Hiring a local guide can truly enhance the experience. They can take you into sites otherwise off-limits to the public.

*Addresses pp. 74, 79, 84, 88 and 92.*



## THE PEARLING PATH ★★★

**E1-3** From Qal'at Bu Mahir to the Siyadi complex, the route is lit by lampposts each fittingly crowned by a lantern in the shape of a pearl. Hard to get lost then along this 2-mile stretch (*p. 34*). Not all the buildings along the route are open to visitors as some are still in the throes of restoration. If you spot someone inside a building, feel free to say hello. The locals are incredibly friendly and may well give you a glimpse inside.

### Qal'at Bu Mahir

**E3** *Daily ex. Tue 9am-6pm - free entry.*
From the 17th c., a fort guarded the route between Manama and Muharraq. It lost its military importance when the island fell under British control in 1862, and today only one of its four corner towers has survived. The structure was the starting point of the pearling expeditions when almost 400 ships would set sail together to spend long months at sea.

### Pearling Path Visitor Center

**E3** *Daily ex. Tue 9am-6pm - free entry. Another Visitor Center in* **D2.**
This is the ideal stop to begin your exploration of Muharraq. A detailed map shows the location of the historic houses. Panels (in English) explain why

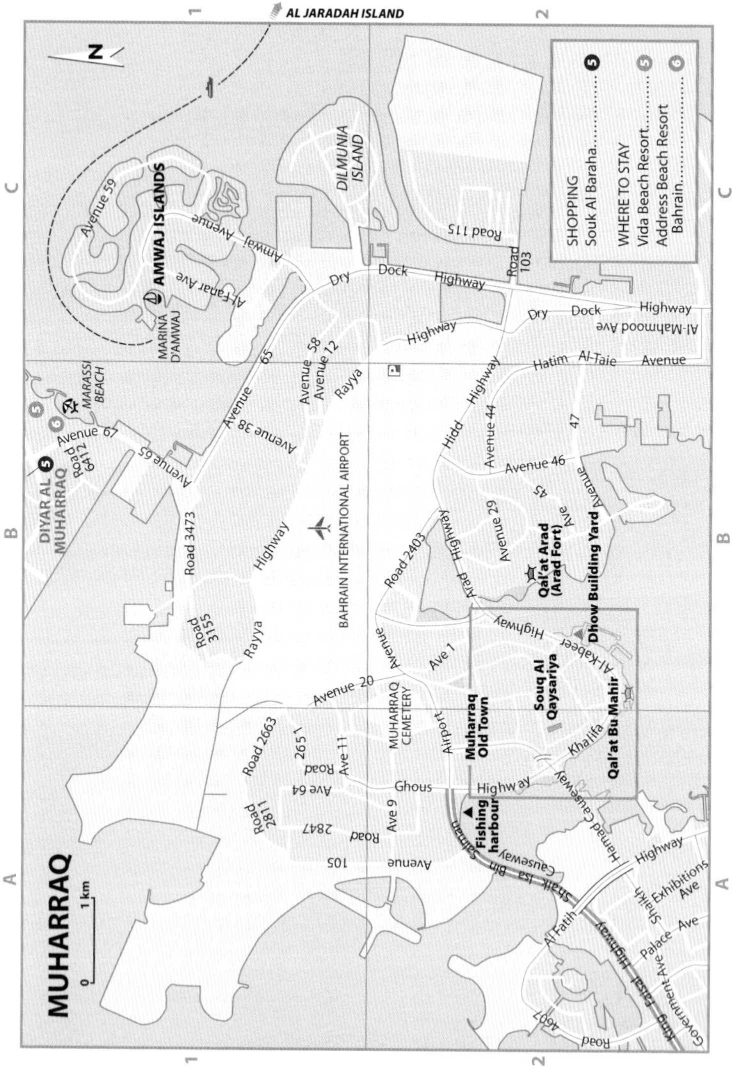
MUHARRAQ
0
1 km
AL JARADAH ISLAND
AMWAJ ISLANDS
MARINA D'AMWAJ
DILMUNIA ISLAND
MARASSI BEACH
DIYAR AL MUHARRAQ
BAHRAIN INTERNATIONAL AIRPORT
MUHARRAQ CEMETERY
Muharraq Old Town
Souq Al Qaysariya
Qal'at Bu Mahir
Dhow Building Yard
Qal'at Arad (Arad Fort)
Fishing harbour
Avenue 59
Amwaj Avenue
Al-Fanar Ave
Dry Dock Highway
Road 115
Road 103
Al-Mahmood Ave
Hatim Al-Taie Avenue
Hidd Highway
Avenue 44
Avenue 46
Avenue 47
Avenue 45
Avenue 29
Arad Highway
Road 2403
Al-Kaber Highway
Avenue 58
Avenue 12
Avenue 65
Avenue 38
Avenue 67
Road 6412
Road 3473
Road 3155
Rayya Highway
Avenue 20
Ave 1
Airport Avenue
Road 2663
Road 2651
Ave 11
Ave 64
Ghous Highway
Khalifa
Road 2811
Road 2847
Ave 9
Avenue 105
Shaik Isa Bin Salman Causeway
Hamad Causeway
Highway
Al Fatih Highway
Shaikh Exhibitions Ave
Palace Ave
Government Ave
King Faisal Highway
Road 4607
SHOPPING
Souk Al Baraha ........ 5
WHERE TO STAY
Vida Beach Resort ........ 5
Address Beach Resort Bahrain ........ 6
A
B
C
1
2

the pearling industry was so important and how the men who plied this trade – sailors, divers, captains, merchants and others – used to live.

## Al Ghous House

**E3** *Rd 1615 - access dependent on any restoration work underway.*
Pearl fishers used to live in this house, adjacent to the port. The modest single-storey structure is composed of three enclosed rooms, although the *liwan* or vaulted portal around the central courtyard would have provided cool respite for the occupants and suggests a certain degree of comfort. When the house was built at the turn of the 20th c., pearl fishers were fairly well-off: it was a time of prosperity courtesy of the pearl, a global export and literally worth its weight in gold.

## Dar Al Muharraq★

**E3** *Rd 1612 - free entry.*
This edifice in the heart of Muharraq's labyrinthine Old City shows what a motivated restoration project can achieve – a triumphant union of heritage and bold modern design. Enveloped by a steel mesh on the outside, inside the structure is a welcoming space fitted out with light wood parquet and slender columns. Design that is the handiwork of Belgian architects Geers-Van Severen. It's a contemporary interpretation of a dar, a traditional place where musicians and singers would come together to perform fijiri, vocal music sung by men at sea (*p. 32*). Reviving the tradition, here musicians gather on the benches arranged along three walls to put on concerts during various annual festivals hosted by the city (Spring of Culture, Muharraq Nights, *Festivals and events p. 104*). When the steel mesh is raised, spectators get watch this rousing performance from the street.

## Badr Ghulum House

**E3** *Lane 1622 - access dependent on any restoration work underway.*
This is the former residence of a folk medicine therapist and barber who set up shop in Muharraq in 1912. On one side of the courtyard you can still see the treatment room where he saw patients and kept his apothecary. The property has preserved its fine *liwan* and several original decorative features.

## Al Jalahma House

**E3** *Lane 1622, next door to the house above - under restoration.*
The interior layout of this opulent residence has been preserved, its complicated arrangement of courtyards and corridors separating reception areas for men and their guests and female-only domains. When the restoration is complete, visitors will get to see decorative stuccowork, wood panelling, stained glass and other ornamental details.

## Nuzul Al Salam

**E2** *Abdulrahman Al Fadhel Ave. - free entry during the day when the hotel is open, usually 8am-7pm.*
This charming boutique hotel was once a handsome family residence in the heart of the Old City. The property

### Fijiri, the pearling fisher blues

Muharraq's pearl fishers and divers gave birth to this traditional form of vocal music in the late 19th c. The repertoire recounts the hardships faced at sea during fishing seasons that would last three to four months. A fijiri performance is composed of five strictly codified sequences of slow, sustained rhythms. The lead singer chants his melancholic refrain ('my beloved, no matter how far apart we are, we will always be close to each other') to which the other musicians respond, beating the rhythm on tambourines or pottery jars, mimicking the gestures of sailors at work. During the more fast-paced sections, some participants might get up and dance. Fijiri are performed on terra firma only. Not that they left the music behind once out at sea: *nihma* were a type of sea shanty sung to encourage work on the boats. Each crew would have had their own singer. While traditional pearl divers are a relic of the past, fijiri continue through classes taught by passionate defenders of the art. These songs were inscribed on the Unesco List of Intangible Cultural Heritage in 2021.



has been fully restored by Bahraini designer Ammar Basheir, and the result is very attractive. True to its original layout, the house is arranged around a large central courtyard (now covered) overlooked by a mezzanine corridor. The decor is particularly pleasing to the eye: bespoke cement tiles mimic this flooring style from the early 20th c. while Italian-designed furniture sits alongside citrus trees conjuring the garden as it might once have looked. The stunning staircase leading to the first floor is made of 700 pieces of oak supported by a metal frame. The six bedrooms combine modern comfort and nods to tradition. The hotel is only available for exclusive hire, ideal for a group of friends or a family looking to stay in a truly authentic setting.

## Al Alawi House

**E2** *Abdulrahman Al Fadhel Ave. - closed temporarily.*

This house was built in 1932 by a wealthy family of merchants who had made their fortune as boat chandlers. The Al Alawi family also delivered drinking water to the fishermen during their long pearling expeditions. The house reflects the family's prosperity, with its two floors, interior courtyard and opulent decoration of which a significant portion has survived. We can't wait to see the finished result once it reopens.

## Fakhro House

**E2** *Shaikh Abdullah bin Hamah Ave. - under restoration.*

Although you can't yet venture inside due to the ongoing work, the site is worth a detour. This elaborate abode belonged to a prosperous trader whose warehouses were located nearby (*p. 36*). Owner of a 50-strong fleet of boats and a timber and materials merchant, Yousif Abdurrahman Fakhro commissioned this small palatial residence composed of two separate buildings (only one of which has survived) set around a

# The Pearling Path

In 2012, Muharraq made it on to the Unesco World Heritage List, crowning a decade of planning and restoration work.

The initial wake-up call came in 2000 when Muharraq was on the verge of dying out. This erstwhile centre of the pearling economy had fallen into disregard from the late 1930s. Merchant families abandoned their beautiful homes; long-standing storehouses collapsed into ruin; a population of poor workers were left to occupy old dwellings that were slowly but surely falling into disrepair. Noura Al Sayed, Director of the Department of Architecture at the Bahraini Ministry of Culture, recalls that: 'The restoration project in Muharraq had two objectives: to improve living conditions for residents, and to preserve the history of the city in which part of Bahrain's national identity had been forged.' One of the first decisions was to set a height restriction on new buildings. A second resolution was to involve residents in the meetings held in the local *majlis*. This was no mean feat given that the creation of 16 squares as envisaged in the project raised more than a few eyebrows – public spaces are not traditional features in the Arab world. They were, however, necessary, otherwise the spaces left vacant by demolished buildings would have been taken over by car parks. After an initial trial, residents embraced the squares, which have become popular spots for people to gather and children to play. In 2023, 17 buildings – modest fisherman's houses and lavish pearl trader's villas alike – were restored impeccably using traditional techniques and materials. But this wasn't all: project designers called too on architects around the globe to bring their own, sometimes radical touch, to the scheme.

Muharraq's conservation can also be attributed to the **Shaikh Ebrahim Center**, working hand-in-hand with the Ministry of Culture. The director of this non-profit organisation founded in 2002, Sheikha Mai bint Mohammed Al Khalifa was a key figure in securing the Pearling Path's status as a World Heritage Site. 'I remember in the 1980s,' she says, 'when the area was in a state of neglect. But the original urban grid and maze of alleys had been preserved, and this worked in our favour. Without that, Unesco wouldn't have accepted it.' Another reason for the positive decision to include Muharraq on the list was its common thread, the pearl – an integral part of the city's identity. This explains why the World Heritage site recognition was extended, at the same time, to three pearling fields off the island's coast as well as to Bu Mahir Fort, from where every year fleets of fishing boats would set sail.

vast garden whose dimensions can still be appreciated today. Much of the original decorative elements (wood panelling, stucco, stained glass) in the remaining structure can be glimpsed from outside. At the time the house was built (early 20th c.), it stood on the waterfront.
*From there either follow the Pearling Path to Murad House or continue ahead to visit Souq Al Qaysariya.*

## Murad House

**E2** *Rd 1308 - free entry.*
With Murad Majlis opposite, this building is a classic example of a pearl trading complex in the Old City: a residence on one side and a guest house separated from the family home on the other. The house is under renovation with plans to turn it into a boutique hotel.

## Jamsheer House

**E2** *Rd 1347 - daily ex. Friday. 9am-noon, 3pm-7pm.*
Privately occupied today, this house is nonetheless open to visitors. A wonderful opportunity to see an authentic period residence dating from 1880 and featuring a handsome courtyard, living spaces and a terrace.
*Return to Murad House to continue along the waymarked Pearling Path.*

## Mohammed bin Faris House of Sut Music

**E2** *Rd 1533 - daily ex. Friday. 8am-2pm, 4pm-7pm - paid entry: Culture Pass* (*p. 103*).
This faithful recreation of a traditional house stands on the exact spot where folk musician Mohammed bin Faris once lived. He achieved fame in the 1930s for updating *sut*, a traditional Bahraini style of bluesy music featuring slow rhythms and nostalgic lyrics. Personal belongings and vinyls pressed in Baghdad or Aleppo bring his successful career to life. Visitors can also listen to recordings of his songs. Just next door (*Block 213; same visiting conditions*), **Mohammed bin Faris Music Hall** honours this music in a beautiful auditorium. A free recital is held every Thursday at 8pm.

### Pocket architecture glossary

**Badgir**: or 'wind catchers' acted as traditional air-conditioning systems (*see box p. 36*).
**Barasti**: small temporary huts built from palm trunks and fronds to provide shade in summer.
**Harem**: domestic spaces reserved for the women and family life.
**Liwan**: a narrow portal often open to the outside, built against the southern wall of domestic courtyards where occupants could enjoy cool air.
**Majlis**: a reception room reserved for male guests hosted by the master of the house. It was the most decorative part of the residence with its own entrance from the street so as not disturb the harem. The wealthiest families would also have had a majlis next to their home.

## Souq Al Qaysariya★

**E2** *Bumaher Ave.*
Muharraq's commercial hub has

been given a radical makeover. In the mid-1800s, this area was where pearl merchants flocked to do trade in the local coffee houses, and captains came to kit out their boats with ropes and sails, not to mention provisions for their crew from the shops brimming with tea, spices and dry goods. Back then, the souq was right on the shore. The district fell into rapid decline from the 1930s, and only the smallest local businesses continued to trade. A regeneration project was launched in 2010. It continued until 2022, under the stewardship of Dutch studio Anne Holtrop. The result is spectacular, with historic buildings having been rescued from dereliction, such as the Siyadi shops *(Tujjar Ave.)* and close by a traditional coffee shop unchanged since 1932, featuring an Indian billiards table. When buildings were dilapidated to the extent that restoration was a no-go, new commercial thoroughfares were constructed. Faithful to the original style, features such as the beautiful wooden store shutters were fitted, but unexpected brutalist concrete elements have modernised the souq to epic proportions. The restored boutiques are now occupied by young designers and craft stores.



## Amarat Fakhro★★

**D2** *Tujjar Ave., opposite the Siyadi shops.*

This collection of storehouses (*amarat*) was once right on the seafront. Deliveries of imported cargo – building timber from India, for example – and shops selling boat paraphernalia would have lined a central alley. The completed restoration of the *amarat* furthest north gives you a good idea of the original layout: a long passageway covered by a high ceiling for better air circulation with shops on both sides. The site was regenerated by Studio Anne Holtrop using its particular treatment of concrete.

Perhaps the most striking feature is the vast béton brut canopy supported by gravity-defying pillars which covers the space where the second storehouse once stood *(daily ex. Sun 10am-5pm).* This structure, making almost no compromise with the local architecture – but for the turrets rising from the roof evocative of traditional wind towers –, is the handiwork of Swiss architect Valerio Olgiati. This sprawling, engulfing space is an impressive sight. On the ground, archaeological digs have

### Natural air-conditioning: wind towers (Badgir)

This ingenious ventilation system invented in Persia was imported to Bahrain at some point in the mid-1800s. The tower has openings near the top designed to capture hot winds: the increase in heat inside the tower causes the hot air to rise, creating an updraught which directs the cooler air from the lower part of the tower toward the dwelling spaces. The system works even when there is no breeze: the air in the tower heated by the sun is enough to create a difference in pressure.

brought to light evidence of ancient occupation – ca. 6th c. AD –, most notably the remains of a date press along with the baskets, which held the fruit, still in place. Beneath the canopy is a **visitor centre** *(same opening hours)*. It houses an exhibition on the local area.

At the end of Tujjar Ave., you'll cross Sh. Hamad Ave., one of the major commercial thoroughfares in the district. Anyone with a sweet tooth should make a beeline for the *halva* specialist, **Hussein Mohamed Showaiter Sweets** (*Addresses p. 84*), and the factory across the road from the shop where this delicacy is manufactured in huge vats.

## Al Darwasa Antiques



**E2** *Rd 1125 - daily ex. Friday.*
This wood-carving workshop is the domain of **Jamal Shaheen**, one of Bahrain's master carpenters. Feel free to step inside to admire models of boats and pieces of furniture in production. Jamal Shaheen has crafted most of the decorative doors that embellish the houses restored as part of the Shaikh Ebrahim Center project. He regularly takes commissions from customers all over the Gulf region.

## Bin Matar House
### (Memory of the Place)

**D1** *Rd 1129 - daily ex. Friday. 8am-1pm, 4pm-7pm - paid entry: Culture Pass.*
This house was erected in 1905 on ground reclaimed from the sea: 'Reclaimed Lands', therefore, are nothing new. It was owned by Salman bin Hussain bin Matar, one of the most prominent pearl merchants of his day. He met Jacques Cartier when the French jeweller made his first trip to Bahrain in 1912. In 1925, he opened Muharraq's first health clinic, under the stewardship of an Indian doctor. Occupied by the family until 2002, the building was painstakingly restored to showcase its original decorative features. Now extended with a modern wing, today it holds art exhibitions. Matar House continues to set the standard in pearl and jewellery trading (*Addresses p. 84*).

## AROUND THE SHAIKH EBRAHIM CENTER★★

**GH2** A handful of royal residences, all closed to visitors, are located in this part of Muharraq. It was here that the new ruling dynasty settled in the 19th century. It is also one of the handsomest areas of the city, its narrow lanes and white-painted houses giving it the air of a medina. *The buildings restored under the aegis of Shaikh Ebrahim are open to visitors daily (ex. Fri) 8am-2pm and 4pm-7pm on presentation of the Culture Pass* (*p. 103*).

## Vertical Garden and Green Corner★

**G2** *Shaikh Abdulla Ave.*
This green wall was erected in 2011 by Patrick Blanc, the French botanist who came up with the concept in 1986, with his first installation at the Museum of Science and Industry in Paris. The

tropical species selected grow up a polyamide felt surface which supports their roots. Next to the Vertical Garden, two spectacular contemporary structures perfectly illustrate the bold regeneration planned for the area. The **Green Corner**, designed by Studio Anne Holtrop, is formed of concrete blocks moulded directly on the ground at the time of construction, lending the building its irregular, geological appearance. It serves as an archival centre for the Shaikh Ebrahim Foundation. During the week, you can ask to look around or even visit the upper floors. Another surprise lies behind the wall: a multi-storey **car park** featuring striking curved slabs designed by Swiss architect Christian Kerez. Three additional car parks in the same style were commissioned for Muharraq to free up the streets from unregulated parking and improve car access for visitors.

## House of Architectural Heritage

**G2** *Lane 918.*

This striking contemporary-design structure was a joint project by two architects: one Palestinian, Noura Al Sayeh, and one Swiss, Leopold Bianchini. The minimalist beam structure framed by the walls of two existing buildings on each side plays host to exhibitions on the local regeneration scheme, its aims and its prospects.

## Abdullah Al Zayed House★

**G2** *Lane 918.*

This house is dedicated to Bahrain's press heritage. It was in this 100-year-old building that Abdullah Al Zayed (1899-1945), writer, poet and pioneer of journalism in Bahrain, lived as well as founded the first weekly newspaper in Bahrain. The beautifully restored

### Muharraq during the pearling age

Every June, Muharraq would burst into a state of nervous excitement as the Ghous Al Kabir – or the Great Dive – approached, signalling the departure for the oyster beds. On the day itself, the whole city would gather at Qal'at Bu Mahir to watch the fleet set off – as many as 400 ships heading off for the fishing season. Depending on the size of the vessel, the crew would range from 10 to 100 men: sailors, divers, the Quran reciter, not to mention the captain and his second in command. On land, the women would serenade the men as they departed. Four months later, the crowd of women would gather again to watch the return of the pearling fleet: Al Quffal. Cries of joy when loved ones made it home mingled with cries of heartbreak when a wife or mother learned that their husband or son had been lost at sea. Every fishing season, Muharraq would be empty of men, bar a handful of elders. It was even said that in some of the poorer quarters, women no longer wore the veil, since any young man they might encounter in the street would still be a child, since he wasn't at sea.

interiors contain displays of souvenirs and records of his life's work.

Opposite the building, the blank wall behind a tall building has become the canvas for a **wall painting** created by French-Tunisian artist eL Seed (*see box p. 42*).

Along the same alley you will also find **Al Nuzul House**, restored as a guest house once more, and the **House of Coffee**: behind the traditional façade lies a vast contemporary space constructed within the walls of three heritage buildings.

## Kurar House

**G2** *Lane 918.*

Every Tuesday, Wednesday and Saturday morning, women skilled in the art of *kurar* come to demonstrate their craft (*see box p. 43*). The mechanisation of the textile industry combined with the cost of this embroidery technique and lifestyle changes almost signalled the end of this ancestral handicraft. With the opening of Kurar House by the Shaikh Ebrahim Center, now the last

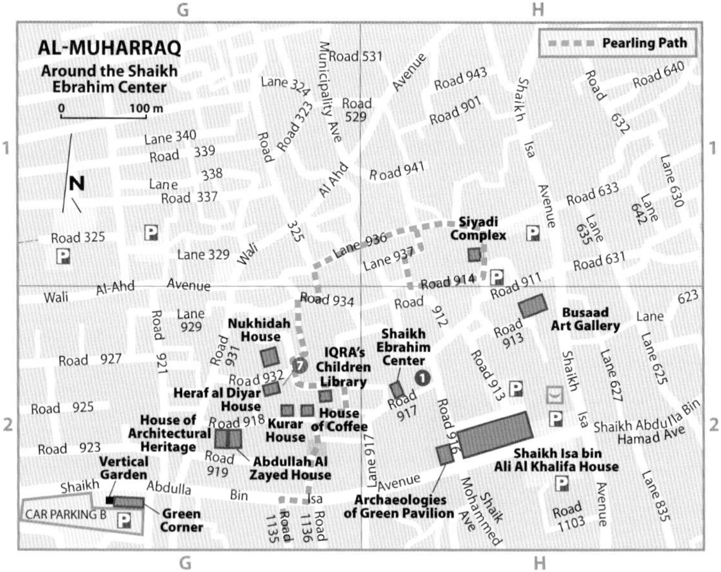


| WHERE TO EAT | WHERE TO DRINK |
|---|---|
| Dona's Wonders ....... 7 | Bu Khalaf Coffee Shop ....... 1 |

**eL Seed, the star calligraffitist**

Born in 1981, the French-Tunisian artist eL Seed, nicknamed the 'calligraffiti artist' early in his career, has carved a name for himself thanks to his large-scale murals, colourful paintings inspired by Arabian calligraphy. His poetic or spiritual messages adorn walls in London, Marseille, Dubai, from favelas in Rio de Janeiro to townships in South Africa by way of villages in Nepal. One of his most spectacular projects is *Perception*, an anamorphic fresco covering almost 50 buildings in Cairo's waste-collecting settlement. Today recognised as one of the most creative contemporary artists of his generation, eL Seed makes a point of involving the local communities in his art projects. He also practises wood carving and glass-blowing, again inspired by the inherent curves and arabesques of calligraphy.

custodians of this art can pass it down to the next generation. The house itself is a fine example of successful restoration.

## Nukhidah House



**G2** *Lane 920 - closed for restoration.*
This 'captain's house' is actually a *majlis*, a separate building where the master of the house would receive and entertain guests. During the restoration, some of the original decorative details were saved and contemporary features were added. A pearl museum is planned for the house with displays of authentic pieces on loan from Bahrain National Museum and the Cartier collection.

## IQRA's Children Library

**G2** *Lane 920.*
This picture-book building in white and blue now houses a library for kids. Readings and play workshops are organised several times a week for the neighbourhood's youngest residents. Inside, lovingly restored period features segue harmoniously with contemporary additions. As you enter, note the beautiful wooden door, crafted by master carpenter Jamal Shaheen (*p. 38*).
Further along this alley, you'll pass **Dona's Wonders**, a perfect spot for coffee and cake or a bite for lunch (*Addresses p. 74*), then **Heraf Al Diyar House**, another restored house which hosts various events organised by the Shaikh Ebrahim Center.

## Shaikh Ebrahim Center★

**H2** *Lane 917.*
This is the nerve centre of the renovation project in historic Muharraq. The foundation's offices and a small heritage exhibition are housed here. The building itself is relatively new, built on the site of a former *majlis* used by the emirs. Here you can also buy the Culture Pass which gives admission to the restored houses open to visitors (*p. 103*).

## Archaeologies of Green Pavilion

**H2** *Rd 916 - daily ex. Wed. 10am-6pm.*
Gardens and orchards have been part of the island's landscape since

ancient times. Here, Studio Anne Holtrop has created its contemporary interpretation: a path snaking through a dozen plant species, either indigenous or from much further afield, including the hardy banana, fig tree, olive tree and lemon tree.
This structure was the Bahrain Pavilion at Milan Expo 2015. It was transported to Muharraq in 2018.

## Shaikh Isa bin Ali Al Khalifa House★

**H2** *Shaikh Abdulla Ave. - under restoration (opening soon, enquire for details).*
When its restoration is completed, this palace will be a key site of interest to anyone visiting historic Muharraq. Erected around 1800, it served as both the emir's residence and the seat of his government. It remained occupied by members of the royal family until 1972. The sprawling complex consists of several rooms arranged around four courtyards that define the different spaces. To the west are the sheikh's apartments. On the first floor, the magnificent decorative features in the summer room have been preserved: graceful arches, a roof of palm tree branches and leaves, stuccowork in the form of geometric motifs... Note the apertures allowing air to circulate. Below the courtyard's eastern wall, a wind tower stands above the *majlis*, the place where the master of the house entertained guests. This is followed by the women's area set around the largest courtyard, then the smallest courtyard where the servants lived, then the area reserved for guests.
It's a maze that you'll be happy to get lost in as you admire the stunning ornamentation and sweeping vistas of the city from the terrace.

## Siyadi Complex★

**H1** *Exterior only.*
The complex in question consists of three buildings constructed by the Siyadis, a wealthy family of pearl merchants. The earliest structure is the mosque (mid-19th c.) with its sumptuous prayer hall (*visitors permitted before prayer time*). To entertain guests outside the family home, the Siyadis built a *majlis*, a stunning four-storey construction whose exterior decoration echoed the grand opulence of its owners. This was where the Siyadi family received pearl traders hailing from Europe or India. The vast palatial residence comprising multiple buildings and courtyards still belongs to the family today.

### Kurar: choreographed embroidery

This traditional craft is the practice of weaving ribbons from gold, silver and silk threads to decorate clothing. The intricate pieces require at least four women to weave the ribbons, and even more for more complex designs. Each woman weaves the threads they are assigned before crossing arms with the women on each side, to build up the weave. One woman sitting opposite tightens the threads to create the final ribbon.

mg81/Getty Images Plus



The Siyadi family's mosque and majlis.

## Busaad Art Gallery

**H2** *Shaikh Isa Ave. - ℘1700 0020 - www.busaad.com - daily ex. Fri. 9am-1pm, 4pm-6pm.*
Art makes a nice excuse to step inside this period house from the 1930s. Ibrahim Busaad (born 1954) is a Bahraini painter and calligraphist who shows a selection of his works here.

# OTHER SIGHTS IN MUHARRAQ

## Dhow Building Yard ★★

**B2** *Rd 1655.*
This is the last surviving building yard specialising in *dhows*, the round-hulled boats you'll often spot sailing in the Arabian Gulf. It's a workshop from another age, with Manama's skyline as the backdrop. The savoir-faire needed to craft a *dhow* is passed down from one generation to the next. The plans are stored in the minds of the carpenters who skilfully replicate the techniques and structures taught by their master, usually a family elder. The keel is built first, followed by the hull supported by scaffolding. The deck comes next. The main wood employed is teak for its exceptional durability. A *dhow* is expected to be seaworthy for 50 years without the need for maintenance. The same can't be said of today's fibreglass models. What about the tools? Nothing has changed

from previous generations: saw, drill, chisel and adze remain standard. It takes 10 months to two years to build a *dhow*, depending on its size. Three workshops share the boatbuilding yard. After offering you a warm welcome, the carpenters will gladly demonstrate their expertise before letting you climb on board a *dhow* under construction.

## Qal'at Arad
### (Arad Fort)

**B2** *Rd 4233 - daily ex. Friday. 9am-5pm.*
This fort still stands as proud as ever. Perhaps not least because it has undergone a complete restoration. The square structure guarded by a circular tower at each corner dates from the late 15th and early 16th c. Originally standing on its own island, it defended the strait between Muharraq and Manama islands. Take a tour to discover its guardrooms and firing posts and clamber on to the ramparts to soak up picturesque **views★** of the Manama skyline and the *dhows* ranged on the shoreline in the foreground.

## Fishing harbour

**A2** *Rd 1715.*
The best time to take a tour of Muharraq's traditional fishing harbour is first thing in the morning. On dry land, fishermen deftly mend their nets and prepare their huge traps which can hold up to 40 kilos of fish while traders expertly eye up the day's catch. For some crews, expeditions out at sea can last as long as a week. The view of Manama's gleaming towers is also worth the trip.

## AMWAJ ISLANDS

**C1** *From Muharraq's Old City, head northwest to the other side of the airport. From Bin Matar or Green Corner, the 7-mile trip takes 25 min. by car.*
The contrast between historic Muharraq and Amwaj Islands is more akin to switching planets than neighbourhoods. You can't help but think of other artificial islands, such as Palm Island in Dubai. But to be fair, any suggestion of imitation ends there as the Bahraini were already reclaiming land from the sea as early as the late 1800s. Amwaj Islands are doing their bit for the country's post-oil economic policy to diversify

The best time to take a tour of Muharraq's traditional fishing harbour is first thing in the morning.

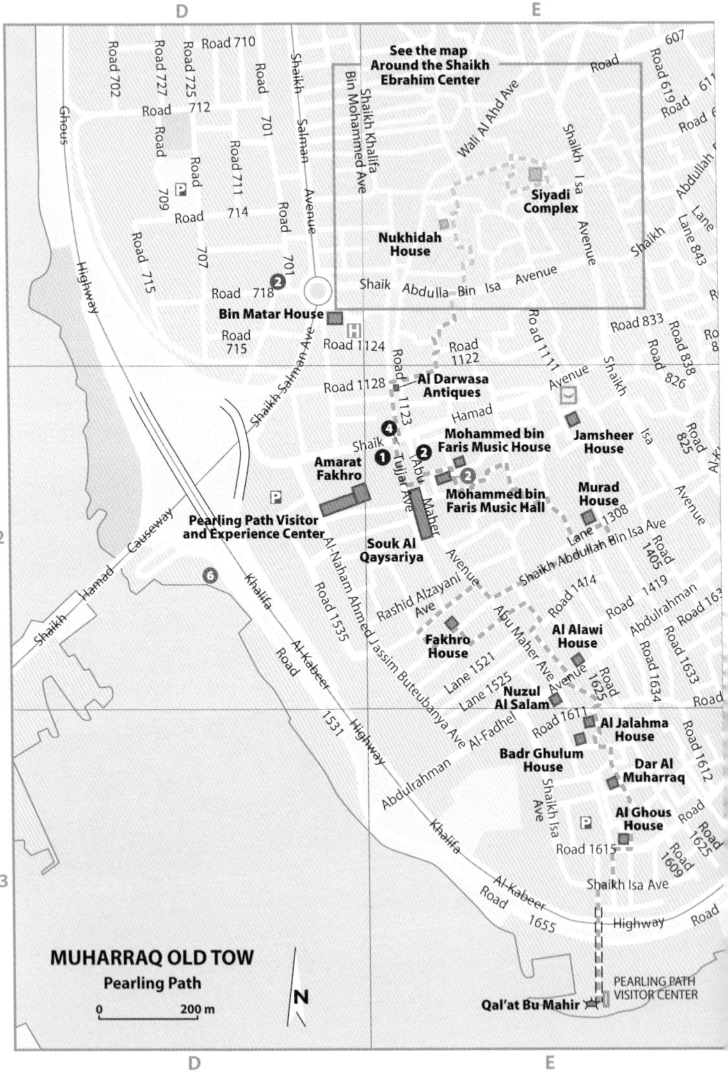

D
E
1
2
3
See the map Around the Shaikh Ebrahim Center
Siyadi Complex
Nukhidah House
Bin Matar House
Al Darwasa Antiques
Mohammed bin Faris Music House
Jamsheer House
Amarat Fakhro
Mohammed bin Faris Music Hall
Murad House
Pearling Path Visitor and Experience Center
Souk Al Qaysariya
Fakhro House
Al Alawi House
Nuzul Al Salam
Al Jalahma House
Badr Ghulum House
Dar Al Muharraq
Al Ghous House
Qal'at Bu Mahir
PEARLING PATH VISITOR CENTER
Shaikh Salman Avenue
Shaikh Khalifa Bin Mohammed Ave
Wali Al Ahd Ave
Shaikh Isa Avenue
Shaik Abdulla Bin Isa Avenue
Shaikh Hamad Causeway
Khalifa Al-Kabeer Highway
Shaikh Abdullah Bin Isa Ave
Abu Maher Ave
Rashid Alzayani Ave
Al-Naham Ahmed Jassim Buteubanya Ave
Abdulrahman Al-Fadhel
Ghous Highway
Road 710
Road 702
Road 727
Road 725
Road 712
Road 701
Road 711
Road 709
Road 714
Road 707
Road 715
Road 718
Road 1124
Road 1122
Road 1128
Road 1123
Road 1111
Road 833
Road 838
Road 826
Road 825
Road 607
Road 619
Lane 843
Lane 1308
Road 1405
Road 1414
Road 1419
Road 1535
Road 1531
Lane 1521
Lane 1525
Road 1611
Road 1625
Road 1634
Road 1633
Road 1612
Road 1615
Road 1609
Road 1655
Shaikh Isa Ave
Highway
MUHARRAQ OLD TOW
Pearling Path
0 200 m
N

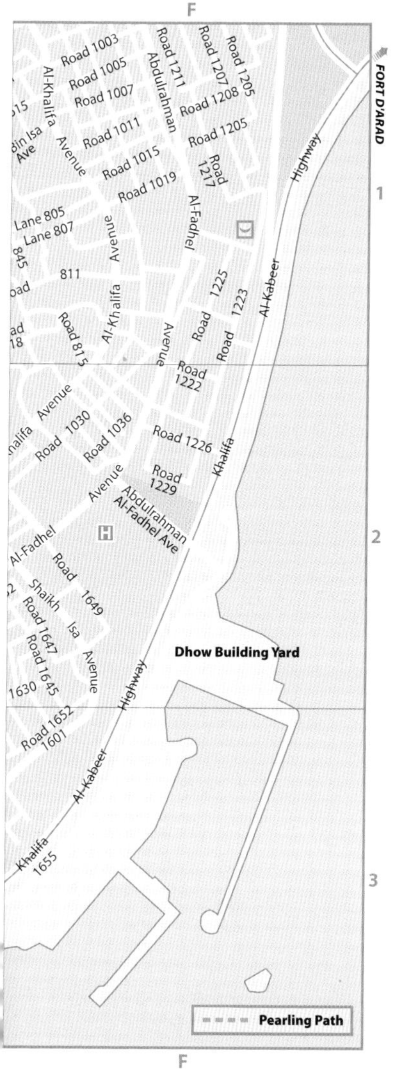


### WHERE TO EAT
Naseef ........ 6

### WHERE TO DRINK
Jasmi's Coffee ........ 2

### SHOPPING
Hussein Mohamed Showaiter Sweets ........ 1
Sophia ........ 2
Alqaysariya Sweets ........ 4

### NIGHTLIFE
Mohammed bin Faris Music Hall ........ 2

into the financial services, real estate and tourism sectors. They were also the first district in the island nation to offer 100% freehold land so expats and overseas investors could own property outright. Here over 1.6 sq. mi you will find everything you'd expect from a waterfront resort: luxury villas and apartments with sea views, upscale hotels, coffee shops and restaurants offering international cuisine, bowling alleys, a shopping mall, beaches, a lagoon... and of course a marina with 145 berths for yachts big and small. Every water sport is catered for, and it is also here where passengers come to embark for the fantastic cruise out to Al Jaradah Island (p. 66).

Amwaj Marina

It is the last remaining building yard for *dhows*, traditional vessels in the Gulf region.

# Northern Governorate ★

**This part of the island beckons you to explore some 4,000 years of Bahraini history. Qal'at Al Bahrain, then known as Dilmun, was a major port in the Arabian Gulf around 2000 BC. Learn about its history during a visit to the museum. Three other sites from the same era complete the tableau: Barbar Temple where cult followers worshipped the god of freshwater; Saar, an archaeological site that gives you a glimpse into the everyday lives of Dilmun's inhabitants; and the amazing royal tombs in A'ali. En route, break up your history tour with a visit to the camel farm which makes for a fun interlude.**

▶ **Getting there:** by bus to Qal'at Al Bahrain; you'll need a car for other parts of the region.

**Detachable map AC2-4.**

▶ **Tip:** set aside a whole day to visit the entire region.

*Our addresses pp. 74, 80 and 85.*



## QAL'AT AL BAHRAIN ★★★

### (Bahrain Fort)

**D2** *Easy to get there from Manama city centre (Bab Al Bahrain) on the number 23 bus; departs hourly, last return 10:40pm, takes 20 min.*
*Start your visit with the museum, free audio guides available.*

An archaeological site of major importance, a modern museum with fascinating displays, and a lovely terrace to watch the sunset: three good reasons to visit!

**Important dates in history.**

The excavations carried out since 1954 and still ongoing have traced the chronology of the site's occupation for almost four millennia.

**2200 - 1800 BC – Dilmun I.** With its moorings protected by the lagoon, the port city becomes an important stopover along the trade routes between India, East Africa and Mesopotamia.

**1700 - 1000 BC – Dilmun II.** After a century of conflict, the city becomes a vassal to the Babylonians.

**1000 - late 4th c. BC.** Assyrian then Persian domination.

**4th c. BC - 7th c. AD.** Known as **Tylos**, the city continues to prosper as a trading hub.

**7th c. AD.** The arrival of Islam. Circa 1000 AD, a fort is built on the ruins of the ancient town near the shore.

**1520 - 1602.** Portuguese occupiers build the fort. By the late 16th c., ships have become too large to enter the port, which falls out of favour. The Portuguese withdraw in 1602. Only a small village remains on the site of the ancient city (*p. 108*).

## The museum

*Daily ex. Mon. 8am-8pm - 2.20 BD.*
An enlightening introduction to gauge the measure of this complex site. The first room presents the mammoth task the archaeologists faced. A cross-section of an excavation trench has been recreated using fragments unearthed on the site, displayed on a concrete structure. Resembling a layer cake, the base dates from the 3rd millennium, and the upper strata from the Islamic period. You can even make out a black line, evidence of a fire. In the same room, you can see a reconstructed traditional fishing boat from Bahrain, still in use until recently and crafted from techniques harking back to the Dilmun civilisation.

The remaining exhibits on the ground floor take you on a journey back in time: ship's anchors and cylinder seals from the turn of the 2nd millennium through to coins struck with the bust of Alexander the Great. Excavations have uncovered a possibly ritual practice unique to the region: during the Persian era (6th - 4th c. BC), snakes were placed in clay pots and buried under houses. Archaeologists have unearthed around 50 of these serpent sepulchres whose significance remains unknown.
The upper level is dedicated to the site's last occupation, from the Islamic Middle Ages to the Portuguese period. Ancient Dilmun continued to be a stopping point along the major

©Eric Sander (ericsander.com)

The Portuguese fort as it would have looked in the 16th century.

maritime trade routes. Chinese coins and pottery have been discovered there. Other relics found (including a wooden spoon and a lute) shed light on how the Portuguese lived inside the fort.

After your visit to the museum, follow the shore around to the fort perched on its mound.

**The waterfront fort**. This square-plan fortification dates from the Islamic Middle Ages, between the 10th and 13th centuries. You can still perfectly make out the base of the walls over 2 m thick and those of the corner towers. Built on the edge of the shoreline, this structure would have served as a storeroom: coins and various fragments of Chinese pottery have been unearthed there. Ascend a small hill for an overall view of the site. On the fort's north side (opposite side from the sea), a trench contains traces of the city walls from between the 3rd and 2nd millennia.

**The Portuguese fort**. *Daily 8am-8pm - free entry.*

The highest point of this imposing fortified town was meticulously restored in the 1990s. The state you see it in today was how it would have looked from the mid-1500s until the Portuguese departed in 1602. Once you pass through the entrance porch, follow an arched passageway to the walkway. Firing posts and defence towers are evocative of its military role. At the north side, take in a sweeping view of the dig site of ancient Dilmun, still under excavation by French archaeologists and so closed to the public. Visitors can go down into the base of the two defence towers housing two unexpected installations by French sculptress Marie-Françoise Rouy: silver gelatin prints displayed on concrete slabs.

After your visit of the fort, return to the museum for a well-deserved rest on the pleasant café terrace (*Addresses p. 80*). The inlet of the ancient harbour lies before you. Low tide reveals the base of the tower flagging the channel which gave access to ships through the coral reef. On the opposite side, a palm grove is suggestive of the lush landscape that once surrounded ancient Dilmun. Today it's a royal property.

## Barbar Temple

**C2** *Daily 8am-5pm - free entry*

The site was first exhumed by a Danish archaeological team in 1954. High walls; blocks of limestone carved from nearby Jidda Island, carefully pointed; a host of religious objects and traces of animal sacrifice: everything points to the site being the largest and most prestigious shrine in ancient Dilmun. The superb bronze bull's head on display at the Bahrain National Museum was discovered here (*photo p. 23*). Three temples were built one upon the other between 2100 and 1900 BC around a natural spring. The sanctuary was dedicated to Enki, the Sumerian god of freshwater. With a little imagination, you can follow in the footsteps of the priests who would have conducted the ceremonies. To the right of the complex, an oval enclosure was used to keep the sacrificial livestock (sheep or goats). The animals would then have been led up a ramp to the entrance of the temple and tethered to stone blocks pierced with a round hole which are still there today. Taken inside the temple to the circular altar, the animals were then ritually slaughtered. Take the stairs below you down to the entrance of the tunnel leading to the holy spring. It was said to communicate with the abzu, the freshwater ocean abode of Enki.

## SAAR

### Saar Archaeological Site

**C3** *Daily 8am-5pm - free entry*
Excavations of ancient Dilmun uncovered its trade port, Barbar Temple and funerary sites. There were gaps on how the island's inhabitants went about their daily lives. These were filled in with the exploration of the Saar site in the 1990s. British archaeologists unearthed the illuminating remains of a village of some 200 houses occupied between 2200 and 1800 BC. From the entrance, a path leads to the village: a main street with side streets running off at right angles. All along it, the street was lined with twin rows of houses. Most dwellings consisted of a main room and one smaller one, used as a storeroom. In some, the oven is still intact, almost identical to the *tannur* used by bakers today. Archaeologists have brought to light all sorts of objects giving a glimpse into the daily lives of this ancient people, from plates and fishing harpoons to jewellery and toys. At the highest point of the village was a temple, its walls still standing at almost 3 metres today: a single small room, its roof supported by three pillars. The benches lining the walls of the temple have survived along with the principal altar, where images of idols would have been placed in front of burning incense. A tiny room would have been used to store liturgical objects.



**Local farmers' market**
This seasonal market, open daily from December to April *(8am-2pm)* in **Budaiya**, is packed with colourful stalls touting all kinds of fruit, veg and herbs. You'll find honey and dates too, while local artisans – potters, weavers, wood carvers – come to demonstrate their talents. One area is taken up by street food vendors and stalls where you can snack on piping hot falafel, Bahraini breakfasts, delicious pastries and more.

## JANABIYA

### Royal Camel Farm

**C3** *2.5 mi southwest of Saar - daily 7am-7pm - free entry.*
This Arabian camel farm was started in 1978 by Sheikh Ibrahim bin Salman Al Khalifa, the uncle of the current monarch. From the initial 24 camels, the farm is today home to almost 400. The camels are not bred for meat or riding but for the sheer pleasure of the royal family who still own the farm today. Enjoy a stroll between the enclosures, guided by farmhands who will happily give you fodder so you can feed these one-humped beasts with your own hands. At the back of the estate to the left is an enclosure reserved for young camels. The ideal spot to take a cute selfie with a baby dromedary.

Basket weaver at Budaiya farmers' market.

# AL JASRA

## Bait Al Jasra

**B3** *Mazarea Hwy - daily ex. Fri 8am-2pm - free entry.*
This fine home from the early 20th c. has been lovingly restored with traditional materials. A royal residence until the 1930s, the current king was born there, in 1933. Explore the courtyards and buildings, a portion of their decorative details and period furniture still visible today. Note the wooden platform outside which provided cool respite during the hottest months.
Five hundred metres north and open to visitors is **Jasra Crafts Training Center** where artisans skilled in all manner of disciplines showcase their talent and creativity (*Addresses p. 85*).

## King Fahd Causeway

**AB3** Completed in 1986, this 15.5-mile causeway connects Bahrain with Saudi Arabia. A series of road bridges spans the gap between the two nations. Visitors can venture as far as the border post on an island bisected by the maritime border that divides the countries. Expect crowds at the end of the week when thousands of Saudi citizens cross the border for a weekend break in Bahrain.
*(You'll need a visa if you want to enter Saudi Arabia. Apply for one online at www.visa.visitsaudi.com.)*

# A'ALI

**CD3** *11 miles southwest of Manama.* There are two main reasons to come this far: its potters and the Dilmun Royal Mounds.

## The pottery village

A'Ali has been Bahrain's pottery centre for generations. In the three large workshops, lined up in a row, visitors get to watch pottery being made and see the enormous kilns where up to 300 objects can be fired in one go. You can even try your hand at making pottery yourself (*Addresses p. 85*).

## Royal Mounds ★

### (Dilmun necropolis)



**CD3** *Free entry.*

These are the most spectacular graves from the Dilmun civilisation. Not least for their size: from the vast scale of the graves compared to the thousands of tumuli dotting the landscape, they are thought to be royal tombs. Mound number 8, fully excavated by a Bahraini team, gives a good idea of the layout of these prestigious structures. The tomb was surrounded by a low stone wall, its carefully pointed base still in place. The tomb itself was cylindrical; a large segment of the exterior wall made of beautiful dressed stone has survived to this day. On the western side *(where you enter)*, a hefty stone door blocks the access to the funeral chamber. Today, entry is made through a gap on the north side: a long passage opening on to six lateral chambers. Digs on the site have unearthed all kinds of funerary relics: stone crockery, ceramics imported from Mesopotamia, ivory... but no bones, the grave having been raided in ancient times. Other equally impressive tombs are located around the village.

**Dilmun Burial Mounds**

The vast number of tumuli harbouring graves has been astounding visitors since the early 19th c. Nearly 170,000, in fact, stud the island's northern and western terrain. Initial thinking put the hillocks down to a rare geological formation until the first digs brought to light graves: a pit covered by a cone of earth and stone shaped into a mound by time and erosion. Since then, the tumuli have drastically dwindled in number due to urban sprawl, although nearly 12,000 of them remain.

A'ali Bahrain's pottery centre for generations.

# Southern Governorate ★

This is the island's largest region: a succession of urban areas, steppe and desert, in the southern-most parts. The central swathe is spiked with oil fields and criss-crossed with pipelines; the west is better preserved. Don't imagine you'll get to see everything in one day. Plan your itinerary around what you're most curious to see. Every interest is catered for: the interactive museum at the National Charter Monument; the sublime Catholic cathedral slap bang in the centre of the steppe; the international Formula 1 racing track; an art gallery... A lovely way to end your day is relaxing on Al Jazair, Bahrain's biggest public beach. A great way to meet the locals.

**Getting there:** Riffa lies 8.5 mi south of Manama city centre.
**Detachable map CE4-8.**
**Getting there:** the distances between the different points of interest mean you'll need your own vehicle.



*Our addresses pp. 76, 80 and 93.*

## RIFFA

The kingdom's second city by population is home to the country's ruling family: in the distance, a giant Bahraini flag marks the spot of the royal palace, unfortunately closed to visitors. You can however wander around the West Riffa neighbourhood to cast your eyes on the royal properties along the wide boulevards nestled in lush greenery. To the east, the historic city sprawls over a hill crowned by a fortress. Lovers of art – and of beautiful buildings – should make a beeline for the RAK Foundation. The city's multitude of cafés and restaurants offer welcome moments of respite.

### Riffa Fort★

**(Sheikh Salman bin Ahmed Al Fateh Fort)**

**D4** *9am-5pm - free entry*
Fort after fort has occupied this site since the 17th c. The surviving one dates from the early 1800s: a handsome military structure protected by high walls and corner towers. It served as the residence of Bahrain's monarchs and the seat of the national government until 1860. Fully restored, the fort makes for a picturesque stroll, the maze of courtyards and staircases leading to countless rooms, some prettily decorated for its former residents, others unadorned, once used as storerooms and defence posts when the fort was in military use. The

terrace affords sweeping views of the island interior. Extend your visit in the bijou café. Within the fort, a modern building houses a small-scale museum (*currently closed*) dedicated to the history of the royal family.

## Military Museum

**D4** *Sun-Thu 8am-1pm - free entry*
Next to the fort, this exhibition tells the history of the Bahraini military forces since the emirate was founded. Bahrain's 14,000-strong army earned an illustrious reputation in various overseas operations. A guide will lead you from room to room and shed light on the collections of weapons and uniforms.

## RAK Foundation★★

**D4** *Villa 231, rd 610 - ☎ 3304 0480 - www.rashidalkhalifa.com - by appointment only.*
Rashid Al Khalifa, born in 1952, is at once a celebrated Bahraini artist – each year his work is shown all over the world – and a collector of contemporary art. In his childhood home, he has assembled hundreds of artworks produced by artists around the globe that speak volumes about the world beyond borders and different cultures. Pieces by 'classic' modern artists, the likes of Yves Klein, Soulages, Bottero, Buffet, César (there's a version in crystal of his lauded sculpture *Thumb*), are shown

The RAK Foundation, where you can admire contemporary art in sublime and serene surroundings.

©Eric Sander (ericsander.com)



Our Lady of Arabia Cathedral serves the kingdom's 80,000 Catholics, mostly Indians and Filipinos.

among works by emerging artists. Admire a small collection by Middle Eastern artists too. The tour – guided only – is fascinating. The building alone is worth the visit: a period home from the 1920s arranged around a central patio where a lush-green ziziphus shrub holds court. The second phase of the building dating from the 1960s is where you'll see Rashid Khalifa's first ever artistic creation: a mural that he painted when he was 14 years old. Not to mention the vast 'white cube' gallery faithful to Yves Klein's concept. In this version, you enter through a splendid wooden door hand-crafted by the star Bahrainin cabinetmaker **Jamal Shaheen** *(p. 38)*. Occupying the patio, an openwork metal cube serves as the founding artist's personal studio.

## AWALI

### The Cathedral of Our Lady of Arabia

**D4** *Rd 403, Block 946 - ✆ 1749 0929 - www.bahraincathedral.org - 8:30am-noon, 3:30pm-8:30pm.*
The octagonal dome in the style of a Bedouin tent has stood in the centre of the steppe since 2021, crowning the Catholic cathedral of the Apostolic Vicariate of Northern Arabia, which encompasses Bahrain, Kuwait and Qatar. It stands on land personally donated by the incumbent king as

a sign of his support in promoting interreligious dialogue. Along with the donation, the vicariate's seat was transferred from Kuwait to Bahrain, home to nearly 80,000 Catholics, the majority Indian and Filipino. The immense space inside the church has capacity for 2,300 worshippers beneath its impressive wooden roof that could have been built by shipwrights. Under the dome, a series of 16 paintings depict the life and passion of Christ. They are faithful reproductions, using high-definition photography techniques, of the murals painted by Spanish artist Kiko Arguello (born in 1939) that adorn San Bartolomeo de Scandicci in Italy. Photographed on canvas, they were then retouched by decorators under Arguello's artistic direction. The artworks, inspired by Byzantine iconography, form a 'crown of mystery' true to the artistic vision of Arguello, who also had an influence on the cathedral's footprint working with the Italian architectural firm commissioned to design the building.
In the corner chapel left of the entrance stands the statue of Our Lady of Arabia, the patron saint of Arabian Catholics.

## National Charter Monument★★

**D4** *Zellaq Hwy - ✆ 1744 7777 - Sun-Thu 7:30am-2:15pm - free admission.*

The Formula One Grand Prix on Sakhir International Circuit in 2023, won by Max Verstappen.

A spiky concrete spire signals the location of this building for miles in every direction. In fact, it's a sun dial that towers over the site, a monument inaugurated in 2010 to commemorate the Bahrainis' approval by referendum of the national charter which led to the institution of a parliamentary monarchy. The exterior walls are engraved with the names of 220,000 citizens enrolled on the electoral lists at the time of the initial consultation. A poignant tribute for the Bahrainis, the place might not warrant the attention of overseas visitors were it not for its engaging museum that narrates the history and achievements of the country. Ten spaces equipped with remarkably well designed interactive displays take you on an immersive journey to discover Bahrain and its people. Take the helm of a merchant ship sailing between Mesopotamia and India to escape pirates in pursuit, storms and sea monsters. Or become a pearl fisher during a virtual dive that will test your ability to hold your breath. In this section, make sure you listen to the speakers playing *fijiri*, traditional vocal music performed by pearling crews and now inscribed on Unesco's Intangible Living Heritage List (*see box p. 32*). You can also get to handle the controls of a Formula One racing car on Sakhir international circuit. Kids will love it and adults will happily play along. One of our top picks.



## SAKHIR

This attraction in the middle of the dessert is a mecca for motorsport fanatics. It's the site of a Formula One track where the Bahrain Grand Prix is competed for each year as well as one of the world's premier karting facilities.

### Sakhir International Circuit

**C5** *www.bahraingp.com.*
The idea to build a Formula One circuit in Bahrain came from Prince Salman bin Hamad Al Khalifa, a huge motorsports enthusiast. Eighteen months and 150 million dollars later, the track was completed on 17 March 2004. The first Formula One Grand Prix in the Middle East took place on 4 April of that year. Since then, the race has become a regular fixture on the world championship calendar. It's generally held in March – at night when it's cooler – and kicks off the F1 season. The country's racing future is looking bright: in February 2022, F1 and Bahrain signed a new deal to host the Grand Prix through to 2036. On top of this major race, the track welcomes a packed programme of events throughout the year (*see calendar on the website*). Not to mention all kinds of activities: tours of the facilities (*by appointment*), from VIP tours with 360-degree circuit views to the track's control centre by way of the stands (*7 BD*); obstacle courses riding in a 4x4; racing in a dragster (*with a*

The Tree of Life the last remnant of the Garden of Eden – as local lore has it

*driver!)* to experience all the thrills and excitement of the 3.363-mile-long circuit. The track is even open from mid-October to April to pedestrians for jogging days!

## International Karting Circuit

**C5** *www.bahrain-karting.com - 10am-11:30pm (Sun-Mon 4pm-11:30pm) - from 14 BD/15 min. - free access to the terrace.*
Just next to its big sister for F1 racing, the karting circuit boasts a champion-worthy track. This high-octane experience is open to all, from the age of 7 up. Simply choose your package and have your photo taken. Each time you complete a lap, your performance will be displayed on the giant screen at the start line, with your name... and face pic! Visitors can watch the racing from the well-appointed terrace.



# OIL FIELDS

## Oil Museum

**D5** *21 mi south of Manama - ☏ 3321 0770 - Fri-Sat 10am-5pm; rest of week by appointment - free entry.*
A fascinating intro to Bahrain's oil history from 1930 – when the first deposit was discovered – to the present day. Exhibits include scores of historical documents, such as the first concession granted to an oil company, and the development of mining technology. Vintage photos around the museum bring the past to life. It's a shame that this compelling attraction isn't open to a wider public. Next to the museum is the first oil well, opened in 1932, and on the other side is the small office where the oil workers would come to pick up their weekly pay packet.

## Tree of Life ★

**E6** *26 mi south of Manama - free admission.*
A solitary pop of green on an otherwise barren hill in the desert, the Tree of Life is an important symbol of Bahrain and for Bahrainis. Legends about the tree's source abound: it is said to have been planted by Enki, the Sumerian god of freshwater, or else to be all that remains of the Garden of Eden. The fact that it manages to survive without a drop of water in sight would indeed seem to be miraculous... were it not for the investigations conducted by scientists. The base of its trunk is surrounded with a series of holes left by core drilling during the dendrochronological survey. It turns out that the tree was planted around 1580 and is a *Prosopis cineraria*, related to the acacia and known as *ghaf* in Saudi Arabia. A characteristic of this species is the ability of its roots to grow deep down into the earth, up to 35 metres, to draw hydration from the water table. The Tree of Life has been helped along the way by fungi growing on its roots, increasing their water absorption. Archaeologists have provided answers too: they unearthed around the tree the remains of a village from the Islamic Period dating from the 14th-16th centuries. You can see traces around the tree's base. This means that the former inhabitants, too, would have had enough water to live here.

©Eric Sander (ericsander.com)

The Heritage Village is open during certain festivities.



While the mystery that shrouds the site has been somewhat lifted today, it doesn't make the sight of this tree soaring dozens of metres into the air in the middle of the desert any less spectacular.

## ASKAR

### Heritage Village

**E5** *Irregular opening hours.*
A wonderful site that deserves a bigger audience. A traditional Bahraini village has been painstakingly reconstructed here along with its souq, mosques, opulent merchants' houses, police station and other typical buildings. Even the riverbank hasn't been overlooked with huts made from palm timber and fronds, where families would come for cool respite during the hottest months of the year. The village is generally only open for the occasion of certain festivals – evenings during Ramadan, for example – or special events. You can always try your luck with one of the ever-present security guards who may let you have a look around.

## ZALLAQ

### Al Jazair Beach

**C6** *24 mi south of Manama - 8am-6pm - 2 BD.*
Bahrain's only fully developed public beach. Along a long strip of fine sand, you'll find all the seaside amenities you'd expect: sunbeds and parasols to hire, water sports equipment (kayaks,

paddleboards, windsurfing boards) and food trucks for a bite to eat and drink through the day. Life guards monitor the beach.

## BAHRAIN'S ISLANDS★

### Al Dar Island

**F4** *www.aldarislands.com - entry 6 BD (children 3 BD), 8/5 BD at weekends.* Just minutes from the coast by boat, this island is home to a resort where you can overnight in a beach hut or a chalet. Day trips possible from Sitra fishing port. Come and relax on the sand, partake in water sports, go out on a boat or just chill. From here, you can also hop over to Al Jaradah Island.

### Al Jaradah Island



**Off map** *Departures from Sitra or Amwaj Islands marina in Muharraq - costs around 110 BD for a 3-hour journey, 6 pers. max.* *(Address book, p. 100).*
Island is a bit misleading for this patch of land that vanishes into the sea at high tide. But it's a fantastic experience not to be missed. Bring the makings of a picnic and the boat crew will provide parasols and a barbecue. You can even stop along the way to go diving.

### Hawar Islands

**GH6-8** This archipelago forms a protected nature reserve to which access is strictly limited. There was a hotel on the main island that organised safaris, but it's now closed, although plans to reopen it are afoot *(enquire)*. South of Bahrain, this group of desert islands is less than a mile from the Qatari coast. The two countries were long in dispute over the sovereignty of the islands until an agreement was reached in 2001; Qatar was granted just one of the islands, the one closest to its shores. The islands were classified a Ramsar site due to the large populations of sea birds, in particular one of the largest concentrations of Socotra cormorants in the world. They're also a refuge for dugongs *(see box below)*.

**The Hawar Islands' dugongs**

A close relative to the manatee, the dugong is a marine mammal that can grow to quite a size: 3-4 m long and weighing up to 500 kg. Dubbed sea cows, they feed on seagrasses which they graze on in shallow waters, near the shores and in lagoons. They number 6-7,000 individuals in the Arabian Gulf with a high concentration of the creatures in Bahraini waters, and especially around the Hawar Islands. A species under threat of extinction, from intensive hunting in the past and by ocean pollution nowadays, the species is today protected in Bahrain thanks to a fishing ban introduced in 1986 followed by the establishment of a protected zone around the Hawar Islands.

# ADDRESSES





Manama Souq.
Philippe Orain/Michelin

# Where to eat

Traditional Bahraini cuisine is truly delicious and fragrant (*p. 135*). Most world cuisines can also be found across the island, and you won't be short on choice whatever you're in the mood for. Since the quality of the culinary scene is an important factor when choosing a travel destination, rest assured that foodies are well catered for with a variety of places to eat throughout the kingdom.

**Find the addresses on our maps using the numbers in the listing (e.g. 1). The coordinates in red (e.g. C2) refer to the detachable map (inside the cover).**

## MANAMA

### Souq - Bab Al Bahrain

**Area map p. 16**

#### Less than 3 BD

1 **Haji's Cafe (Haji Gahwa)** – **E1** - *150 Road nº 471, Bab Al Bahrain - 973 1721 0647 - www.instagram.com/hajiscafe/- daily 5:30am-9pm.* This Manama Souq institution founded in 1950 is the place to go and experience a traditional Bahraini breakfast. Fill your belly with a wide range of dishes made to share: beans with eggs, omelette, *keema* and *dal* mix (lamb and pea curry with lentils), *labneh* (strained yoghurt), broad beans, chicken or beef *nashef* and *Machboos* (spiced chicken with rice) to name but a few. The cuisine is hyperlocal, the owner running his own farm producing milk, cheese, veg and other ingredients on the menu. Sitting at one of the tables along a bustling souq alley adds to the charm.

#### 10-30 BD

8 **Indigo Terrace** – **E1** - *150 Government Ave., Bab Al Bahrain - 973 1667 8666 - www.themerchanthouse.bh - daily.* This is the rooftop restaurant of **The Merchant House** hotel (*p. 90*). The modern, artsy decor in the covered dining room is juxtaposed by the outdoor terrace with its British-inspired floral garden reminiscent of a Laura Ashley print. The staff are attentive. The international menu is peppered with local notes. A special mention goes to the lamb shank and the grilled hamour, a white fish from the Gulf.

### Bahrain Bay

**Area map pp. 24-25**

#### 5-10 BD

13 **Lumee** – **C1** - *The Avenues Mall, Seafront, Bahrain Bay - 973 1748 4555 - www.lumeestreet.com - daily 8:30am-11:30pm.* The street food menu at this contemporary café and deli spans the Middle East from Lebanon to Bahrain by way of Egypt and Oman. Expect excellent value for money and dishes bursting with colour and flavour.

#### 30-50 BD

3 **Fish Market Restaurant** – **C1** - *Bldg 587, Road 4613, Bahrain Bay - 973 1710 0800 - www.instagram.com/*

©Eric Sander (ericsander.com)

Haji's Cafe, a Manama Souq institution and ideal intro to the Bahraini breakfast.

*fishmarketbah/- daily noon-11pm.* This stylish and welcoming restaurant is located along the waterfront promenade in the heart of Bahrain Bay. The menu leans mostly fish and shellfish. Diners are invited to compose their own seafood platter from the fresh daily catch presented on the main counter. Everything is then weighed and prepared to your fancy, in a lemon butter sauce, grilled, cooked in parsley or steamed. A real treat!

(14) **CUT by Wolfgang Puck – C1** - *Four Seasons Hotel Bahrain Bay - ✆ 973 1711 5044 - wolfgangpuck.com/dining/cut-bahrain - 12:30pm-3pm, 7pm-11pm.* After Washington DC, Beverly Hills and Singapore, Michelin-starred chef **Wolfgang Puck** has brought his celebrated steakhouse concept to Bahrain, inside the **Four Seasons Hotel** *(p. 91)*. The stunning location, appetising menu and reasonable fixed-price lunch menu entice tourists and business diners alike. The cherry on top: the terrace looking over the hotel pool and lush gardens affords sweeping views of the bay and the Manama skyline.

## Diplomatic Area

### Area map pp. 24-25

#### 5-10 BD

(9) **Darseen Cafe – C2** - *2209 Block 322, Bldg 455 - ✆ 973 7733 6600 - www.darseencafebahrain.com - 9am-5pm, closed Tue.* This charming

café is located inside the National Museum (p. 22). The breakfast through lunch menu offers a delicious selection of Bahraini classics with Indian and international influences. Vegetarian options available. The terrace has lovely views of the bay and the National Theatre next door.

## Block 338

**Area map pp. 24-25**

### 10-30 BD

⑮ **Gunaydin** – **C3** - *Block 338, Bldg 115C, Road 3803, Adliya - 973 1700 0099 - www.gunaydinbahrain.com - Sun-Thu noon-2pm, Fri-Sat 9am-2pm.* The Turkish specialities come in generous portions and each dish is as delicious as the next. A succulent selection of grilled meats. In addition to the standard menu, you can choose from the aged steaks priced at 33-69 BD, including the famous 1 kg Tomahawk to share. Warm atmosphere, efficient and friendly service. Save some room for the *katmer*, a traditional dessert made from sweet puff pastry filled with crushed pistachios and ice cream.



⑯ **Clay** – **C3** - *The Terminal, Block 338, Bldg 120, 5th Floor, Yousif Ahmed Al Shirawi Road, Adliya - 973 1755 4545 - www.claybahrain.com - 12:30pm-1am, Wed-Fri 12:30pm-2:30am.* Nestled on the 5th floor of an anonymous building towering over the trendy Block 338 neighbourhood, this fusion restaurant in an elegant art deco style brilliantly showcases the finesse and technical prowess of Japanese cuisine blended with the flavours of Peruvian gastronomy. The selection of sharing plates and individual dishes is a delight for the eyes and the palate from starter to dessert. Creative cocktails and a great wine and spirits selection. Hip, stylish clientele. Terrace with views over Manama. Lounge music during the week and DJs spinning on weekend evenings.

### 30-50 BD

④ **Fusions by Tala** – **C3** - *Gulf Hotel Bahrain, Block 338, Adliya - 973 1774 6427 - www.gulfhotelbahrain.com/Fusions %20by %20Tala - Mon-Fri 5pm-11pm, Sat noon-5pm - closed Sun - à la carte or tasting menu (39 BD).* Created and helmed by the incredibly talented chef **Tala Bashmi** (p. 138), a star on the Bahraini food scene. Intimate and inviting, this restaurant features among MENA's finest. Gastronomes and gourmets are singing the praises of this restaurant that is without doubt the hottest eating spot in the kingdom. Whether you opt for the tasting or à la carte menu, the brilliantly devised 'fusion' dishes combine local produce, Bahraini flavours and world influences. The creativity on the plate is sheer delight for foodies. The kitchen is surrounded by windows, so guests can observe the deft hand and technical skill of the chef and her team. Forty covers in the dining room plus 70 on the terrace, weather permitting. By reservation only.

⑰ **L'Orto** – **C3** - *Block 338, Bldg 119, Road 3931, Adliya - 973 1777 7818 - www.instagram.com/lorto.bh/ - Sun-Wed 7pm-midnight,*

*Thu-Sat 9am-3pm, 7pm-midnight.* This minimalist contemporary restaurant has a gorgeous, shaded terrace decked out with olive and lemon trees and bougainvillea, giving diners a taste of Tuscany. Here the chef **Susy Massetti** concocts authentic Italian dishes using fresh, carefully selected ingredients. From pizza and pasta to risotto, meat and fish, refined Tuscan cuisine has found a home in the heart of Manama. The ambience is chic and relaxed. Attracts a clientele of regulars. By reservation only, including for the weekend brunch.

⑱ **Mahonia – C3** - *Block 338, bldg 1078, Road 3832, Adliya - ✆ 973 3722 2244 - www.mahoniabh.com - 6pm-2am - à la carte and tasting menu (45 BD).* Bahraini restaurateur **Sawsan Baluch** doesn't hit a single false note at this fine-dining establishment that is possibly one of the biggest culinary surprises in the kingdom. It's a symphony for the senses. For the eyes first, with its glamorous, sophisticated and art-forward decor. Then for the nose and palate, of course, thanks to the meticulously sourced ingredients from the finest local and international producers. Under her orchestration, the kitchen team is as precise as a ballet troupe. The result? Ravishing plates of food and a spectrum of unexpected flavours. An extraordinary culinary experience in every respect.

## Al Seef

**Area map pp. 24-25**

### 5-10 BD

⑩ **Pickl – A2** - *Al'Aali Mall outside entrance, Al Seef - www.eatpickl.com/bh - Sun-Wed noon-1am, Thu-Sat noon-2am.* The retro neon sign of this fast-food chain is a familiar sight across the Gulf. On the menu: chicken, beef and veggie burgers packed with a choice of toppings and a drizzle of secret sauce, hot or not. Burger fans won't be disappointed.

⑪ **Baker & Spice – A2** - *Al'Aali Mall ground floor, Al Seef - www.bakerandspiceme.com - daily 8am-11:30pm.* This all-in-one café, restaurant and bakery where every item is made on the premises uses only fresh, local, organic and seasonal ingredients. The sustainable and fair-trade philosophy is well promoted by the owners; the cheerful staff are helpful. Daily batches of baguettes, fresh bread and pastries. Also serves salads, sandwiches, individual meals and a fixed-price menu for 9.90 BD.

### 10-30 BD

⑫ **Cantina Kahlo – A1-2** - *Ritz Carlton Bahrain, Bldg 173, Road 2803, Block 428, Al Seef - ✆ 973 1758 6401 - www.ritzcarlton.com/en/hotels/middle-east/bahrain/dining/cantina-kahlo - Mon-Thu 4pm-midnight, Fri-Sat 12:30pm-1am, closed Sun.* Taking its cue from the vibrant and eclectic world of artist Frida Kahlo, this eatery pays tribute to the authentic cuisine of her native Mexico. The menu has all the Mexican classics – tacos, ceviche, grilled steak and seafood – along with some original house specialities including *pollo con mole*, chicken with peanut sauce: simply divine. A unique selection of tequilas, colourful and creative cocktails and an excellent wine list.

## Khamis

**Area map pp. 24-25**

### 5-10 BD

(19) **Tabreez Restaurant** – **A3** - *Bldg 50, Road n° 376, Ain Adhari Ave., South Sehla - ✆ 973 1740 6206 - tabreez-restaurant.business.site - 11am-11:30pm, Fri 12:30pm-11:30pm.* A popular haunt with Bahrainis, this simple restaurant has a huge garden usually thronged with regulars. They come for the traditional cuisine and especially the grilled, locally caught fish which is delicious. Servings are generous, the service friendly. The local clientele is usually mostly male, depending on the time of day.

## MUHARRAQ



**Area map pp. 40, 46-47**

### 5-10 BD

(6) **Naseef** – **D2** - *Shop 1, Bldg 1128, Road 1531 - www.instagram.com/naseefrestaurant - daily 8am-midnight.* Set on the boardwalk running along the bay, this restaurant specialises in Bahraini cuisine. While it has an excellent rep for its typical breakfast that is a big draw for locals, it is equally well known for its lamb and chicken dishes and artisanal ice creams with original flavours such as rose and saffron. The most popular though is mango, and for good reason: yum! It has a second outpost in Manama Souq.

♥ (7) **Dona's Wonders** – **G2** - *Road 932 - ✆ 973 1721 3669 - www.donaswonders.com - 8am-7pm.* This cosy gem of a place behind a pretty green wooden door is down a side street in the old town. Find a table in the interior courtyard or the adjoining dining room and soak up the Bahraini boho decor. Owner and chef **Dona** has created a healthy and sublime menu infused with local flavours. She is a big pastry fan too, and her Paris-Brest comes in the classic praline and chocolate version as well as her Middle Eastern take on this French speciality, flavoured with pistachio. Order the house non-alcoholic cocktail and if you can guess the secret ingredient, it's taken off your bill! The hospitality is adorable and the address is still under the radar, just how we like it.

## NORTHERN GOVERNORATE

**Detachable map**

## Saar

### 10-30 BD

♥ (20) **Villa Mamas** – **C3** - *Block 533, Road 3374, Bldg 1856, Al Markh, Saar - ✆ 973 1730 5031 - www.villamamas.com - Sun-Wed 1pm-10pm, Thu-Sat noon-midnight.* Step into this white-painted villa bordered by a garden of palm trees, flower pots and wooden tables in a calm residential neighbourhood and you'd be forgiven for thinking this was a private home. Exactly the reaction that chef and owner of the premises **Roaya Saleh** is aiming for. Inspired by her international travels and deeply attached to Bahraini culture, her food is a delightful homage to her country and the wider Middle and Far East. Expect fresh juices followed by generous starters and mains in which spices and milder flavours vie for attention, all made

Fusion restaurant Clay offers a sublime blend of Japanese and Peruvian cuisines

CLAY

with local, organic ingredients. The waft of fragrant aromas fills the space, and every mouthful transports you to another destination. A treat from starter through dessert. The restaurant is popular with local residents and Saudi travellers in the know – and rightly so.

### Janabiya

#### 10-30 BD

(21) **Aldar Cafe** – **C3** - *District 1 Mall, Janabiya - www.aldarcafe.com - Sun-Wed 9am-1am, Thu-Sat 9am-2am.* This traditional eatery in the modern setting of **District 1 Mall** serves Turkish-Lebanese dishes with the odd nod to India. From the afternoon until late, locals come to relax on the terrace and enjoy a tea and shisha. The traditional-meets-modern vibes apply to the decor too.

(22) **Petiole** – **C3** - *District 1 Mall, Janabiya - www.petiolefoods.com - Sun-Wed 2pm-10pm, Thu-Sat 3pm-11pm.* This attractive concept store promotes a vegetarian/vegan lifestyle in its ground-floor organic, waste/plastic-free store where everything is recycled and/or recyclable. Upstairs, the restaurant celebrates all things plant-based. The owner, **Khalid**, stocks a range of food and non-food products that are kind to the environment. The creative, healthy, tasty and seasonal menu is sure to satisfy committed veggies and sway hesitant ones. The freshly made cocktails are mixed using fruit, flowers and plants. Hats off to this eco-responsible initiative that includes a space devoted to hydroponic farming where the chef grows fresh herbs and garden vegetables soil-free.

### Hamala

#### 5-10 BD

(25) **Plant Cafe** – **C3** - *Shop 84, Road 1401, Block 1014, Liwan Hamala - ✆ 973 3800 7780 - www.plantcafe.co - Wed-Mon 10am-10pm, closed Tue.* The first 100% vegan establishment to open on the island. The Scandi vibes of this café are soothing. All the items, including gluten-free options, are made using fruit and veg. The mouthwatering menu featuring appetising, vibrant dishes, far from being restrictive, is sure to entice even the most hardened carnivore. A shoutout for the *shakshuka* and the avocado, pepper and roast pumpkin on toast. The most sceptical diners only need order the *shawarma*, where sliced meat is replaced with roasted mushrooms and fresh herbs, to be won over by the delights a plant-based diet can offer.

## SOUTHERN GOVERNORATE

**Detachable map**

### Riffa

#### 5-10 BD

(23) **Graffiti Burger** – **D4** - *Mashtan Road - www.instagram.com/graffitiburger.bh/- Sat-Wed 1pm-2am, Thu-Fri 1pm-3am.* This fast-food outlet where as you'd expect the decor is floor to ceiling street art serves hefty, hand-crafted burgers, hot dogs (a rare treat on the island) and even a gourmet version of the Philly cheesesteak!

### 10-30 BD

(24) **My Cafe** – **D4** - *Bldg 259, Road 1405, Rafa Mall - 973 7734 4443 - www.mycafebh.com - daily 8am-11pm.* A chic and casual destination sporting contemporary design with art deco flourishes. At the helm is **Sawsan Baluch**, the Bahraini restaurateur who also brought us **Mahonia** in the capital (*p. 73*). The international cuisine is sprinkled with Bahraini, Indian and Mediterranean notes. The burrata, tomato and roast peach salad, the grilled octopus, and the roasted pumpkin with preserved citrus are all worth a special mention. Draws a regular family crowd. Brunch and afternoon tea are especially popular with locals. Safer to book.

(28) **Grande Caffe Del Teatro** - **D4** -*82 Ajirah Ave - Mon-Sat 8am-5pm.* An 8-minute walk from the RAK Foundation, this trattoria-style eatery is unmistakably Italian with the decor an homage to the *commedia dell'arte*, Harlequin and Venetian masks. The pasta dishes are irresistible as well as easy on the wallet.

## Zallaq

### 10-30 BD

(26) **Zahrat Al Fayrouz** – **C7** - *Jumeirah Gulf of Bahrain Resort & Spa, Zallaq - 973 3366 3466 - www.jumeirah.com/dine/bahrain/zahrat-al-fayrouz - 12:30pm-11pm, closed Tue - Shisha Lounge 2pm-4pm, 6pm-11pm.* On the sea front and set within the superb **Jumeirah Gulf of Bahrain Resort & Spa** (*p. 93*), this restaurant has a beautiful contemporary Arabian-styled dining room and a sprawling terrace beside the pool, a lovely spot from autumn to spring. The menu is a nod to the Lebanon and the wider Middle East, and the dishes are both generous and flavour-packed. Choose from salads, *meze*, and meat and fish prepared in the best Levantine tradition. A special shoutout goes to the Jordanian *mansaf*, lamb cooked in fermented yoghurt and spices, served with rice. Vegetarian options also available. If shisha isn't your bag, ask for a non-smoking table on the terrace.

### 30-50 BD

(27) **Maison Sushi** – **C5** - *Sofitel Bahrain Thalassa Sea & Spa, Zallaq - 973 1763 6912 - restaurantsandbars.accor.com/en/restaurant/6722_R002 - 7pm-11pm, closed Mon.* This stunning restaurant within the **Sofitel** resort sits at the end of a jetty, affording panoramic vistas of the sea. As you might have guessed, the menu is Japanese, not to mention modern and elevated. Think sushi, maki, sashimi, wagyu beef, fish and shellfish *teppanyaki*. The desserts are beautifully dainty. The house cocktail list based on sake (5-7 BD) is accompanied by a selection of Japanese beers plus spirits and liqueurs from around the world.

# Where to drink

From welcoming terraces at trendy coffee houses through juice and cocktail bars to elegant, cosy tea rooms, Bahrain has an abundance of spots to enjoy afternoon tea and cake or a pre-dinner aperitif. Whether your preferred tipple is a traditional cardamom-infused coffee, a fresh fruit smoothie, an Indian-style karak tea or a hand-crafted cocktail shaken by a tattooed mixologist, there's a venue and a beverage to suit every hour of the day.

**Find the addresses on our maps using the numbers in the listing (e.g. 1). The coordinates in red (e.g. C2) refer to the detachable map (inside the cover).**

## MANAMA

### Souq - Bab Al Bahrain

**Area map p. 16**

#### Tea and coffee shop



3 **The Dot Coffee** – **E1** - *Bahrain Post Museum, 2nd Floor, Bab Al Bahrain - www.thedotcoffee.com - 9am-6pm, Sat 9am-9pm, closed Fri. and in summer.* Located on the 2nd floor of the **Post Office Museum** (*p. 14*), this coffee house boasts a lovely patio with views of the **Bab Al Bahrain** building and the souq entrance. Caffeine aficionados are well catered for here with coffees imported from fair-trade roasters in Africa, Asia and Latin America. Cookies, cakes and other treats too.

From 7:30pm on Saturday, score a table on the terrace to catch a free folk music concert held on the square below.

### Bahrain Bay

**Area map pp. 24-25**

#### Tea and coffee houses

4 **The Orangery** – **C1** - *The Avenues Mall, Seafront, Bahrain Bay - www.orangeryme.com - daily 8am-10pm.* Instantly evocative of elegant tea rooms in Paris, London and Vienna, The Orangery is sheer luxury. The pastry counter with a beautiful selection of delectable cakes and desserts is sure to tempt you. Also on the menu, an assortment of macarons and savoury items from breakfast through to dinner. In the afternoon, families and young women are a familiar sight at teatime after scouring the shops in the neighbouring mall. Weather permitting, plump for a table on the gorgeous terrace affording panoramic views over Bahrain Bay.

5 **Bay View Lounge** – **C1** - *Four Seasons Hotel Bahrain Bay - www.fourseasons.com/bahrain/dining/lounges - Sat-Wed 11am-midnight, Thu-Fri 11am-1am.* Set in the luxuriant surroundings of the **Four Seasons** (*p. 91*), this sprawling lounge is adjacent to the lobby of this hotel where guests come to experience ultimate refinement. A place of floor-to-ceiling elegance embellished with olive trees and sublime floral displays; the impeccable service comes with a smile. The menu offers light dishes,

salads and mains. The much-acclaimed afternoon tea is served daily from 3pm. A selection of premium teas is accompanied by wellness juices, original flavoured milkshakes, alcohol-free cocktails and inventive iced teas.

## Al Seef

**Area map pp. 24-25**

### Tea and coffee house

6 **La Reine Cafe – B2** - *El Balcon Mall, Bldg 3214, 346 Road 4654 - www.lareine-bh.com - Sat-Wed 7am-midnight, Thu-Fri 7am-1am.* If the baroque decor, crystal chandelier, velvet couch and fleur de lys motifs weren't clue enough, the 'reine' referred to here is Marie-Antoinette! While she may not have said 'let them eat cake', these would surely have been the gateaux and pastries she had in mind. The all-butter shortbread biscuits, madeleines and mini financiers are a further nod to the decadence of the Court of Versailles. There's also a savoury menu for brunch and other times of day.

### Cigar lounge

7 **Burlington Club – A2** - *The Ritz Carlton Bahrain, Road 40, Block 428, Al Seef - www.ritzcarlton.com/en/hotels/bahrz-the-ritz-carlton-bahrain/dining/- daily 1pm-2am.* From the moment you set foot inside, it oozes the sophistication of a classic British gentlemen's club, with the important exception that women are, of course, welcome! This beautiful, cosy bar features red-leather club chairs and a lounge with fireplace and library. The decor is impeccable, the hushed atmosphere wonderfully relaxing. The free-standing humidor is stocked with a premium selection where true aficionados are certain to find the finest cigars from Havana. From 8pm Monday through Saturday, a singing duet with piano perform live.

## MUHARRAQ

**Area map pp. 40, 46-47**

### Coffee shop

1 **Bu Khalaf Coffee Shop – H2** - *7J36+ PVG, Road nº 917 - daily 8am-12:30pm, 4pm-9pm. Tucked away in the old town, this pint-sized café founded in 1920 was the first to open in Bahrain.* And it's just as popular today! Press cuttings, vintage photos and period decor remind us of its roots and bring the history of this authentic place to life. Serves traditional Arabian coffee or the famous *karak*, a milky tea found all over the Gulf, both infused with cardamom. Located close to the **Shaikh Ebrahim bin Mohammed Al Khalifa Center**, the café is the ideal stop for a caffeine hit along your tour of the historic **Pearling Path** (*p. 34*).

2 **Jasmi's Coffee – D1** - *Bldg 574, Road 718, Block 207 - www.jasmis.com/jasmis-coffee - daily 8am-midnight.* This café chain was founded by two brothers who developed a love of American-style coffee houses while studying overseas. On their return home, they wanted to replicate the model in a way that reflected Bahrain. The beans are all sourced from organic farmers. The menu includes hot americanos and lattes as well as chilled frappés, milkshakes and smoothies. On the back of their success, the menu has

grown, now extending to a wide range of savoury and sweet items. With dozens of branches across the country, the group is committed to social responsibility and charity, for instance making donations to good causes and organising beach clean-ups. The management also encourages its employees and customers to live an active lifestyle: by connecting to the Walk to Eat app, the customer who walks the most number of steps can claim a free meal!

## NORTHERN GOVERNORATE

**Detachable map**

### Qal'at Al Bahrain

#### Coffee shop and bar



**8 GB Cafe Qal'at by Green Bar – D2** - *Road 3863, Seef Area, Karbabad, Qal'at Al Bahrain - www.greenbarinc.com/pages/gb-cafe - daily 7am-midnight.* This eco-conscious coffee shop and bar at the entrance to the **Bahrain Fort museum** (*p. 50*) *serves nothing but local organic products and ethically sourced coffees and teas.* Everything on the seasonal menu from breakfast to dinner is made from scratch.
Head here later in the day, after your museum and fort visit. Find a spot on the pretty outdoor terrace for a front-row seat to watch the sun setting over the sea.

### Janabiya

#### Tea and coffee shop

**9 Rue Catering Boutique – C3** - *District 1 Mall, Janabiya - www.instagram.com/rue.catering - 9am-midnight, closed Sun.* On the back of its excellent reputation across the island, this high-end caterer opened up a lovely bakery to serve its delicious gourmet food and refreshments to a wider audience. On the menu: beautifully presented savoury bites, lip-smacking cakes in individual and sharing sizes, and a selection of pastries, premium teas and coffees and freshly pressed juices. The atmosphere is cosy, the staff friendly and helpful. Residents have already picked up on this delightful address that isn't (yet!) flooded with tourists.

## SOUTHERN GOVERNORATE

**Detachable map**

### Riffa

#### Restaurant and coffee shop

**10 Oak – D4** - *Road 4225, opposite Al Malaki Hospital - www.oak-bh.com - daily 7am-11pm.* In soothing decor dominated by light wood, white surfaces and greenery punctuated by splashes of colour, this coffee house serves from breakfast to dinner an assortment of teas, coffees, smoothies and other hot and cold beverages, a full menu of sweet and savoury items, and bread freshly baked daily on the premises. Vegetarian and gluten-free options available. The chef, where possible, uses local, organic products sourced from farmers' markets or directly from producers on the island. Her dishes incorporate Arabian and Middle Eastern ingredients, including sesame seeds, dates, pistachios, honey, rose and pomegranates.

**11 Roast Coffee Roastery – D3** - *Abu Shahin Ave., across from the Al Reem Centre - www.roastbh.com -*

©Eric Sander (ericsander.com)

GB Cafe Qal'at by Green Bar, the best time to go is late in the day so you can watch the beautiful sunset from the terrace.

*daily 7:30am-11pm.* A friendly coffee house much appreciated by residents and students attending Riffa's universities. Sourced from places such as Ethiopia, Brazil, Colombia and Honduras, all the beans are roasted on site. The full menu covers breakfast through dinner with savoury and sweet items and light refreshments. Other tempting options include cakes, brioche bread, bowls, and smoothies made from acai berries, dates, honey and matcha.

### Chocolates

12 **Leaves – D4** - *Al Raya Mall, Bldg 261, Road 1405, Block 914, Mashtan Ave. - www.instagram.com/cafebyleaves/- daily 2pm-11pm.* Established in 2005, Leaves is Bahrain's premier chocolatier. All its chocolates are hand-crafted from cocoa beans specially selected by a compact team of artisan chocolate makers. They are then shaped and customised by expert designers before being sold by the piece, in boxes, or in gift packs. The shop, of course, offers an assortment of chocolates, but it also has a pastry counter brimming with treats that are as scrumptious as they look. Delectable chocolate tarts and original inventions made from chocolate, hazelnuts, pistachios and caramel can be enjoyed with a piping coffee, tea or, for an extra cocoa hit, hot chocolate. Relaxing music performed live on the terrace from 7:30 pm every Thursday.

# Shopping

Shopping is a favourite pastime among Bahrain's local population as it is across the Gulf region. It's common to see families and friends meet up after work or at weekends in the country's many sprawling air-conditioned malls and shopping centres that offer a tantalising choice of retailers, restaurants, ice-cream parlours and even live music. Travellers will find almost every international brand, although the fun lies in discovering Bahraini labels and designers.

In Manama, Muharraq and the main metropolitan areas around the island, plenty of shops also stock traditional items and local arts and crafts. Popping up more and more are farmers' markets and local producers, as well as places selling spices, perfumes and, of course, such oriental delights as dates, honey, rose syrup, confectionery and other delicacies. Our top tip: save some room in your suitcase!

**Find the addresses on our maps using the numbers in the listing (e.g. 1). The coordinates in red (e.g. C2) refer to the detachable map (inside the cover).**

## MANAMA



### Souq - Bab Al Bahrain

**Area map p. 16**

6 **Made in Bahrain Gift Shop** – **E1** - *Manama Souq, Bab Al Bahrain - Sat-Thu 9am-1pm, 4pm-9pm, Fri 5pm-9pm.* Located along the main alley of the souq, this attractive store is dedicated, as its name suggests, to Bahraini arts and crafts. Pore over accessories, small leather goods, decorative objects, perfumery, costume jewellery, stationery and more: you'll be guaranteed to find a souvenir or two to take home, with the assurance that they are all produced in the island country.

7 **Kingdom of Perfumes** – **EF1** - *Manama Souq, 6HJG+ GJ4, Sh Abdulla Ave., Bab Al Bahrain - Sat-Thu. 9am-1pm, 4pm-9pm, Fri. 4pm-9pm.* A hit with visitors, Kingdom of Perfumes stocks all the international best-sellers. But the big draw here is the array of locally produced fragrances made using aromatic ingredients from the region including rose, musk, oud wood and amber. These scents are deeply rooted in Bahraini traditions and hospitality.

8 **Gold City** – **E1** - *6HMF+ 25G, Government Ave. - www.goldcitymall.com - 10am-9:30pm, Fri 4pm-10pm.* Bahrain's biggest gold market is also home to purveyors of precious gems and metals – from silver and platinum to diamonds and pearls. Merchants sell their wares by weight or by the carat based on prices set by the stock exchange. Authenticity certificates are issued. A reasonable amount of haggling is expected, there's an abundance of choice, and you can even snap up a gold ingot!

### Bahrain Bay

**Area map pp. 24-25**

The Avenues Mall, one of the chicest shopping experiences in Manama.



❾ **The Avenues Mall** – **C1-2** - *Road 4660, Bldg 3977, Bahrain Bay - www.the-avenues.com/bahrain/en - Sat-Wed 10am-10pm, Thu-Fri 10am-midnight.* Stretching along the public promenade, it's the only waterfront shopping centre on the bay. Modern, high-ceilinged and flooded with sunlight, the mall is pleasant to wander around. There are dozens upon dozens of retail spaces and restaurants, some with outdoor terraces where you can relax facing the sea.

## Central Business District

**Area map pp. 24-25**

❿ **Moda Mall** – **C2** - *Bahrain World Trade Center Gate 2 - www.modabahrain.com - daily 10am-10pm.* The most fashion-forward shopping mall in the kingdom where all the major luxury brands (Gucci, Hermès, Dior, Cartier, Audemars Piguet to name but a few) are represented. Italian designers, French fashion labels and Swiss watchmakers have boutiques here. Not to mention premium Bahraini brands like perfumer **Alkashka** specialising in oriental scents. Plus **Asia Jewellers**, established in 1962 by a Bahraini jewellery family, which in addition to jewels by famous houses proposes modern pieces by the talented **Mayyan Jaffar**, the founder's daughter, in her precious jewellery collection, MJ by Mayyan.

## Al Seef

**Area map pp. 24-25**

**11 The Bahrain Mall** – **A2** - *Ave. 28 Bldg 184, Block 410 Sanabis - thebahrainmall.business.site - 10am-10pm, Fri-Sat 10am-midnight.* In the architectural style of an Arabian fortress, this is one of the largest shopping centres in the capital, featuring an American-style food court and hypermarket.

**12 Al Aali Mall** – **A2** - *Road n° 2819, Seef - www.alaalimall.com - daily 10am-10pm.* This shopping centre is one of our top picks because it features predominantly brands from Bahrain and the wider Gulf region, covering jewellery, fashion, accessories, footwear and more. Our favourite brands include **Cult 8 and Mimosa** for female fashion, and the fine boutique **Gaia**, a Bahraini brand of top-of-the-range leather goods, bags, accessories and shoes, all very elegant and affordable. Not to forget the historic **Mattar Jewelers**, a house of jewellery for over a century, renowned for its creations adorned with the famous natural pearls of Bahrain.



# MUHARRAQ

## Old City

**Area map pp. 46-47**

**1 Hussein Mohamed Showaiter Sweets** – **E2** - *Shaikh Hamad Ave., Muharraq Souq - www.instagram.com/showaiter_sweets_bh - daily 8am-10pm.* The kingdom's iconic confectionery store was established way back in 1850! Bahrainis and tourists flock here throughout the day for the famous *halva*, a sweet made from a thick sesame paste and flavoured with rosewater, saffron, cardamom and dried fruit, enjoyed warm or at room temperature. Other treats to take away include almond or pistachio nougat (around 2-4 BD per 500g box).

**2 Sophia** – **E2** - *Tujjar Ave., Muharraq Souq - www.instagram.com/sophia.bahrain - 9am-2pm, 4pm-9pm, Fri 4pm-10pm.* This modern bookshop is hard to miss among the traditional market stalls of the souq. Floor-to-ceiling béton brut walls are offset by wooden shelves and contemporary calligraphy artworks. Publications and glossy magazines in English and Arabic are spread over both floors. Various nooks with benches and footstools provide cosy spaces for customers to flick through books on display. There's a small coffee shop on the first floor. The terrace looks over **Mohammed bin Faris Music Hall** (*p. 35*).

**4 Alqaysariya Sweets** – **E2** - *Road 1553, Block 215, Tujjar Ave., Muharraq Souq- www.instagram.com/alqaysariya_sweets - 10am-2pm, 4pm-9pm, Fri 4pm-10pm.* A tiny but well-stocked family-run shop. You'll find sweets, spices, honey, dried fruits and cakes galore. The syrupy confectionery flavoured with saffron and rose is all made on the premises. One of few retailers to stock packs of ground Arabian coffee infused with cardamom and saffron, from Bahraini brand Raslan.

## Diyar Al Muharraq

**Area map p. 30**

**5 Al Baraha Souq– B1** - *Diyar Al Muharraq/Marassi - www.souqalbaraha.com - 10am-10pm, Fri 4pm-10pm.* The authentic souq experience in a brand-new, single-level contemporary shopping centre. Several coffee shops and restaurants. A farmers' market is held daily from midday to 3pm in one of the courtyards.

## NORTHERN GOVERNORATE

**Detachable map**

### Budaiya

**13 Farmers' Market – C2** - *Budaiya Botanical Gardens - www.instagram.com/farmersbh/- Sat 8am-2pm, Dec to Apr.* This delightful farmers' market set inside Budaiya Botanical Gardens was a government initiative set up in 2012 to promote Bahraini agriculture and artisanship. Over a decade later, it's still going just as strong today! What could be better than pootling about the colourful stalls of a farmers' market, watching weavers and tanners ply their craft, and mixing with the locals doing their market shopping. Take away delicious honey from producers **Helyon Honey** or dates from the **Al Noor** farm. You can also order from one of the food trucks and tuck into your breakfast or brunch in the green space popular with families.

### Al Jasra

**16 Al Jasra Crafts Training Center – B3** - *1003 Road n° 315 - 8am-5pm, closed Fri and Sat.* Arranged around a shady garden, the workshop-boutiques at this handicrafts centre showcase the various disciplines within Bahrain's long-established arts and crafts industry. Basket weaving, ironwork, woodwork, pottery, sewing and other talents are all on show, with visitors able to observe the artisans at work and ask them questions about their practice. The shops are enclosed and air-conditioned so comfortable to visit all year round. If you're looking for souvenirs, the site has a 'Made in Bahrain' store similar to the one at the souq in Manama *(see p. 82)*.

### A'Ali

**14 Green Bar – D3** - *Shop 32 Riyadat Mall, Bldg 231 - www.greenbarinc.com - 9am-6pm, closed Fri.* A 100% organic, environmentally aware Bahraini brand promoting beauty rituals from around the Arabian Peninsula. The products are made from natural plant and fruit oils sourced from the brand's own garden or local farms. Reawaken your senses with date, rose, almond and mint.

**15 Jaffar Mohammed Al Shughul Pottery Workshop – D3** - *Hwy 71, Road 4239, Block 742 - www.instagram.com/pottery_alshugel/- 8am-6pm, closed Fri.* Established in 1949, this pottery workshop is one of the oldest and most highly respected in the kingdom. Watch as potters operate their wheels in the courtyard where just-fired vases, pots, plates and other wares dry in the sun. You get to see the whole intricate pottery-making process, from wheel throwing and firing to glazing and painting. Everything is done by hand. Workshops open to the public are a chance to try your hand at pottery yourself *(3 BD for a 1-hour class).*

# Nightlife

Much like its people, a night out in Manama is vibrant and inviting. Tourists can go and sip a cocktail or order a glass of wine in many of the hotels, restaurants, bars and lounges around the city. Generally speaking, cocktails cost between 5 and 8 BD while a bottle, depending on your chosen tipple, will set you back 25 to 65 BD. But keep an eye on the prices as champagne and fine bottles of wine can ramp up the bill to eye-watering heights.

From Thursday evenings, the cities are especially thronged with travellers from neighbouring countries – predominantly Saudis, Kuwaitis and Emiratis – visiting for the weekend. After dinner, soak up the electrifying atmosphere as you explore the pulsating and pleasant ambiance Bahraini nights have to offer.

**Find the addresses on our maps using the numbers in the listing (e.g. 1). The coordinates in red (e.g. C2) refer to the detachable map (inside the cover).**

## MANAMA



### Souq - Bab Al Bahrain

**Area map p. 16**

#### Bar and rooftop

4 **Alto – F1** - *Downtown Rotana - 110 Government Ave. - 973 1721 0550 - www.thealtolounge.com - daily 5pm-2am.* This city-centre rooftop bar on the 25th floor of the **Downtown Rotana** hotel offers sweeping panoramic views of Bab Al Bahrain and the surrounding neighbourhoods. The lively crowd is a mix of tourists, business travellers and residents. Expect a friendly atmosphere. The selection of international wines and champagnes, cocktails and spirits is accompanied by an à la carte menu. Music every evening, the genre dependent on the DJ that night. Weekends are especially popular with afro-beat, hip-hop and R&B pumping out on Saturdays.

©Eric Sander (ericsander.com)

Halo Lounge, the favourite rooftop haunt of the capital's golden youth.

Bahrain National Theater, a stunning building designed by the French agency, Architecture-Studio.



## Bahrain Bay

**Area map pp. 24-25**

### Bar

**8 Blue Moon Lounge by Wolfgang Puck – C1** - *Four Seasons Hotel, Bahrain Bay - ☎ 973 1711 5046 - www.fourseasons.com/bahrain/dining/lounges/blue_moon_lounge_by_wolfgang_puck - Wed-Fri 6pm-2am, Sat-Wed 6pm-midnight, Sun 12:30pm-midnight, closed Mon.* Conceived by Austrian-American chef Wolfgang Puck who puts his contemporary spin on Moroccan design, this fancy 50th-floor bar and lounge in the **Four Seasons** towers above Manama. The cocktails are inventive and the Japanese snacking menu exquisite. The venue is a firm favourite among Saudi patrons and international travellers, so booking is recommended. Non-smokers should be aware that smoking is permitted inside the panoramic bar.

## Diplomatic Area

**Area map pp. 24-25**

### Classical music, opera, ballet

**3 Bahrain National Theater– C2** - *Shaikh Hamad Causeway - ☎ 973 1729 8 777 - www.culture.gov.bh/en/authority/cultural_sites/BahrainNationalTheatre.* The home of the Bahrain Philharmonic Orchestra is one of the capital's most iconic buildings (*see p. 26*). The main theatre – its 1,001 seats a nod to the Arabic folk tale collection *One Thousand*

*and One Nights* – puts on an eclectic programme: live music and classical ballet, operas, plays and world music with Arabian sounds featuring heavily. Visit the website to view the programme and book tickets.

## Block 338

### Area map pp. 24-25

#### Bars and rooftops

**5 Iris – C3** - *Road 3832, Bldg 1078, Block 338, Adliya - ✆ 973 1721 2223 - www.irisbahrain.com - 6pm-2am, closed Sun.* Oozing style and glamour, this bar and rooftop is set above the splendid restaurant **Mahonia** (*☞ p. 73*). The place is popular with the chic and executive crowd. From early evening onwards, lounge music accompanies a cocktail among friends or an evening meal, where the inventive cuisine is oohed and aahed over in an atmosphere of unbuttoned elegance. From 9pm the atmosphere builds to a crescendo as well-known DJs spin all genres of music until close.

**6 Halo Lounge – C3** - *Road 3819, Bldg 571, Block 338, Adliya - ✆ 973 3690 6900 - www.instagram.com/halobahrain/- Sat-Tue 6pm-2am, Wed-Thu 6pm-3am, Fri 6pm-4am.* The favourite haunt of the 25-40-year-old demographic. The beautiful young things from the countries of the Gulf, along with expats, travellers and the entire generation ofmillennials come here to party the night away. This open-air rooftop bar glowing under a pink neon sign on the plant wall has a DJ, friendly staff, hip clientele, shisha lounge and original cocktails. A nightclubbing formula that hits all the right notes.

**7 Gallery 21 – C3** - *Road 3801, Bldg 21, Block 338, Adliya - ✆ 973 1771 1600 - www.gallery21bahrain.com - daily noon-2am, happy hours 5pm-8pm.* Gallery 21 is a hospitality concept venue composed of a modern art gallery, Moroccan restaurant and lounge, a second Mediterranean- and Lebanon-influenced eatery, and **Mai Tai**, a Polynesian-inspired tiki bar. Classic cocktails and more original concoctions from 7 BD. Party vibes all week long from 9pm with male and female DJs at the decks playing electro-fusion plus Latin salsa and bachata nights and live music.

## MUHARRAQ

### Area map pp. 46-47

#### Folk music

**2 Mohammed bin Faris Music Hall – E2** - *Close to Mohammed bin Faris Music House - www.shaikhebrahimcenter.org/en/houses/bin-faris-house-for-sut-music-2 - Sat-Thu 8am-1pm, 4pm-7pm.* Opened in 2005, this music hall was built as a homage to the Bahraini singer and musician Mohammed bin Faris (*☞ p. 35*). The artiste was a master of *sut*, popular music originating from the Gulf region blending melody, poetry and spirituality. His command of the discipline and his lyrical compositions introduced the genre to a wider audience, while lending it a particularly Bahraini flavour. The venue has an auditorium for hosting artistic conferences and performances. Free folk concerts are held every Thursday evening until closing time.

Gallery 21, a social hub consisting of a contemporary art gallery, two restaurants and a bar.

GALLERY
21
Restaurant&
WE ♥ 338

# Where to stay

Modern hotels, luxury apartments, family-friendly establishments and sublime seafront resorts... Bahrain has every type of accommodation covered, with new developments always on the horizon. Whether you're going for a short city break before jetting off to another destination, a longer stay to explore the country's rich culture, history and cuisine, or simply a holiday to make the most of the beach and the translucent waters lapping the island, there's sure to be a perfect place for you to stay.

**Find the addresses on our maps using the numbers in the listing (e.g. 1). The coordinates in red (e.g. C2) refer to the detachable map (inside the cover).**

## MANAMA

### Souq - Bab Al Bahrain

**Area map p. 16**

**75-140 BD**



1 **The Merchant House** – **E1** - *150 Government Ave., Bab Al Bahrain - ☎ 973 1667 1000 - www.themerchanthouse.bh - 46 rooms.* Ideally located in central Manama, this boutique hotel occupies its own category of unique! A stunning fusion of contemporary design and top-drawer elegance, this establishment takes its art seriously, with modern and contemporary pieces on display in the lobby and on every floor, including works by some of the biggest names in the art world today. It offers 46 suites (no classic rooms), a sublime library, coffee lounge, rooftop restaurant, the **Indigo Terrace** (*p. 70*), and a rooftop pool. The staff are welcoming and attentive, and the atmosphere is intimate and designed to make you feel good from the moment you cross the threshold. It's a hotel with its own unique cachet.

### Bahrain Bay

**Area map pp. 24-25**

**45-70 BD**

7 **Hilton Garden Inn** – **C1** - *Bldg 4091, Road 4661, Bahrain Bay - ☎ 973 7790 1111 - www.hilton.com/en/hotels/bahtagi-hilton-garden-inn-bahrain-bay - 192 rooms and suites.* Attached to **The Avenues shopping mall** (*p. 83*) by an external walkway, this hotel towers over Bahrain Bay. The rooms are bright and spacious, the views varied depending on where you stay. Includes restaurants, a café and fitness facilities. The pool deck on the second floor offers superb views over the emerald waters of the bay.

**75-140 BD**

8 **Wyndham Grand Manama** – **C1** - *Bldg 316, Road 4609, Seafront, Bahrain Bay - ☎ 973 1711 6116 - www.wyndhamhotels.com - 263 rooms.* Instantly recognisable by its sleek

twisted steel-and-glass structure, this luxury hotel takes centre stage in Manama's Bahrain Bay (*p. 20*). The interior is sheer elegance, and the well-appointed rooms decorated with wood, marble, leather and other premium materials are spacious, even if they vary in size owing to the building's circular design. Two pools with bay views, a fitness centre and a lovely spa. Several restaurants, a café-bakery and a bar. The service is pleasant and professional.

**145-300 BD**

② **Four Seasons Hotel Bahrain Bay** – **C1** - *Road 4606, Bldg 555, Block 346 - ✆ 973 1711 5000 - www.fourseasons.com/bahrain/- 273 rooms.* This strikingly modern building towering 201 metres above the bay has an enigmatic H-shaped design that instantly draws the eye. The Four Seasons is much more than an architectural feat standing on its own private island ringed by beautifully landscaped gardens.
The contemporary interiors featuring art deco touches blend seamlessly with Bahraini and Arabian design motifs. The lobby decked out with lush olive trees is flooded with natural light through its sweeping panoramic windows. The atmosphere is serene and sophisticated but never stuffy.

The Merchant House, ideally located in downtown Manama, close to the souq.

The lobby is also where one of the most coveted afternoon teas in the capital is served (**Bay View Lounge** *p. 78*). On the top floor, Skypod is home to the panoramic restaurant and rooftop bar **Blue Moon Lounge by Wolfgang Puck** (*p. 87*), the Michelin-starred chef also behind the acclaimed steak restaurant **CUT** on the 1st floor (*p. 71*). The leisure facilities are up to the high standards you'd expect from a Four Seasons: stunning pools including one for children, a private beach lined with palm trees, and a sublime spa.

## Diplomatic Area

**Area map pp. 24-25**

### 45-70 BD

3 **Novotel Al Dana Resort and Spa** – **D1-2** - *121 Shaikh Hamad Causeway - 973 1729 8008 - all.accor.com/hotel/3600/index.en.shtml - 130 rooms and suites.* Situated on the causeway that connects Manama and Muharraq, this resort hotel has its own private sandy beach and boasts superb views across the capital's skyline. The location, close to the Bahrain National Museum and National Theatre, is ideal for going out to explore Manama's souq and Muharraq Old City (you will need a taxi or CHAUFFEURED VEHICLE to get to these sites). The traditional Bahraini architecture with its wind towers invites families into an authentic setting while promising up-to-date amenities that will entertain the children and pep up the parents: two pools (one for the youngest guests), restaurants including a grill on the terrace, a bar, a fitness centre and kids' clubs.

## Al Seef

**Area map pp. 24-25**

### 145-300 BD

4 **Ritz-Carlton Bahrain** – **A2** - *King Mohammed VI Ave., Al Seef District - 973 1758 0000 - www.ritzcarlton.com/en/hotels/middle-east/bahrain - 245 rooms and suites plus 23 villas with private swimming pool and lifestyle butler's service.* Setting the standard for the ultimate hotel experience, this establishment has lost count of the accolades garnered for its level of luxury and service. On the shores of a picturesque lagoon with emerald water and its own private beach, appealing pool, relaxing spa, superb gardens and ponds where flamingos roam freely, travellers will instantly feel comfortable and cocooned from the outside world, despite being moments away from the bustle of Manama. Choose from several bars, including one of our top picks, the **Burlington Club** (*p. 79*). And a dozen cafés and restaurants, not least **Table Krug by Y**, an epicurean journey for the senses curated by **French executive chef Yann Bernard Lejard**; the modern steakhouse **Plums** and **Cantina Kahlo**, the new Mexican restaurant (*p. 73*).

# MUHARRAQ

## Diyar Al Muharraq

**Area map p. 30**

### 45-70 BD

5 **Vida Beach Resort** – **B1** - *Bldg 176, Road 6403, Block 264, Marassi Beach - 973 7748 8888 - www.vidahotels.com/en/resorts/*

*vida-beach-resort-marassi-al-bahrain - 299 rooms.* Located northeast of the capital, in the up-and-coming hospitality hub **Marassi Beach**, this resort opened to guests in late 2022. The interiors of the rooms and suites, some with sea views, are in soothing natural wood and blue tones. The restaurant **Origins** serves Mediterranean cuisine. Pool plus access to the beach and the seafront promenade at **Marassi Park** where events and festivals take place.

### 75-140 BD

6 **Address Beach Resort Bahrain – B1** - *Marassi Al Bahrain, Block 264, Bldg 176, Road 6403 - 973 7799 8888 - www.addresshotels.com/en/resorts/address-beach-resort-bahrain - 117 rooms and suites.* The high-end twin of the neighbouring Vida Beach, this boutique hotel opened in December 2022. The atmosphere is elegant, the colour scheme marine, the personnel charming. The grand but intimate guest amenities include a café and lounge serving afternoon tea, an internationally inspired restaurant, a fitness centre , and a gorgeous spa. Outside there's a restaurant and shisha lounge, terrace with pool and bar, kids' splash pad and pool, and direct access to a private beach along the Marassi shoreline equipped with sun loungers and beach huts.

Two other establishments under the same brand are adjacent to this resort. Likewise, there is the **Marassi Galleria**, a shopping mall housing shops, restaurants, cafés, ice cream parlours and family leisure amenities, slated to open in late 2023.

## SOUTHERN GOVERNORATE

**Detachable map**

## Zallaq

### 145-300 BD

9 **Jumeirah Gulf of Bahrain Resort and Spa – C7** - *150 Government Ave., Bab Al Bahrain - 973 7777 1000 - www.jumeirah.com/en/stay/bahrain/jumeirah-gulf-of-bahrain-resort-and-spa - 196 rooms and suites.* This 5-star establishment of understated luxury, which opened its doors in early 2023, is situated on the island's west coast, by the turquoise waters of the Gulf of Bahrain, a 35-min. drive from Manama. The hotel atmosphere is inspired by the history of the kingdom, the curves and design evocative of the Arabian Gulf, the ivory and mother-of-pearl tones an obvious nod to Bahrain's famous pearls. The lobby, dotted with pieces of modern art, features a panoramic window letting light flood in and affording stunning sea views, and adjoins a coffee lounge and library. In addition to the hotel, the resort offers 11 villas each with a beach-facing private pool. The lagoon pool is the epicentre of the landscaped grounds and home to Lebanese restaurant **Zahrat Al Fayrouz** (*p. 77*) and Italian eatery **Due Mari**. On the Venetian-style canal surrounding the resort, guests can go for a ride in an *abra*, traditional wooden boats from the Gulf region. The private beach is exquisite, the ocean fauna and crystal-clear water extraordinary. Last but not least, the **Talise Spa** is arguably one of the most stunning on the island.

# PLANNING YOUR TRIP

## Know before you go



## Basic information



## Festivals and events



Bab Al Bahrain, historical building dating to the British protectorate.
Philippe Orain/Michelin

# Know before you go

## Entry requirements

### Passport and visas

British,Canadian, American and Australian tourists must hold a valid passport for the duration of their stay. A tourist visa is issued on arrival: the fee is 5 BD ($13.25) for a 14-day stay, 12 BD ($32) for one month (valid for three months allowing multiple entries). Travellers can apply for an eVisa in advance (for an additional application fee of 4 BD ($11) which can be extended if your initial request is successful. Info: www.evisa.gov.bh
No vaccinations required.



### Customs

The following items can be imported duty-free (or purchased on arrival):
400 cigarettes (or 250g of tobacco);
3 litres of alcoholic beverages;
50 cigars.
No restrictions on imports of local or foreign currencies.

## Getting to Bahrain

Gulf Air is the only airline to operate direct flights to Bahrain, from London Heathrow to Manama, which takes around 7 hours. Flights with one stopover also run from New York JFK, Los Angeles and Sydney. Other airlines operate non-direct flights only, including from Canada.

## Useful addresses

**Embassy of Bahrain in the U.S.** – 1255 23rd St. Northwest, Washington DC 20037- ✆202 342 1111 - www.mofa.gov.bh.
**Embassy of Bahrain in the United Kingdom** – 30 Belgrave Square, London SW1X 8QB - ✆0207 201 9170 - www.mofa.gov.bh.
There is no diplomatic representation of Bahrain in Canada or Australia. Find out more at www.mofa.gov.bh

## Money

The local currency is the **Bahraini dinar** (BHD, locally called BD – pronounced 'bidi'), which is divided into 1,000 fils. Notes come in ½, 1, 5, 10 and 20 BD denominations and coins in 5, 10, 25, 50 and 100 fils pieces. 1 BD = approx. 2.65 USD, 3.54 CAD, 2.09 GBP, 4.06 AUD (August 2023)

### Payment methods

Bank cards are widely accepted, even by neighbourhood shops and taxis. You can find plenty of ATMs in the capital Manama, in shopping malls and around the main towns and cities.

## Budget

Bahrain isn't a particularly low-cost destination on a Western budget.

### Accommodation

Depending on the season, expect to pay $90-210 a night for a double room in a 3- or 4-star hotel and $220-700 in a 5-star or luxury establishment.

### Eating out

A three-course meal at a restaurant in a souq or in Muharraq Old City costs in the region of $11-13 per person. At more upmarket places, expect to pay around $22-38 per person. In the trendier establishments, the bill can be as much as $45 per person for lunch and $65-90 a head for dinner. A meal at a fine-dining restaurant will set you back $110-330. The cost of a cocktail on a rooftop in Block 338 is $20-22.

### Entry fees

Admission to most places to visit is free. When it's not, the entry fee is between $2.80-8.20.

### Transport

A bus ticket costs around $0.70. A taxi fare in the city will be around $13.

## Climate and seasons

Bahrain has two seasons: winter from November to April and summer from May to October, which is extremely hot, so winter is the ideal season for visiting the country. Temperatures from December to February are mild (20-22°C), rising to 26-32°C in October-November and April.
The sea temperature never falls below 20°C. Most rainfall occurs in winter, but rarely more than for a few hours at a time so it's unlikely to disturb your stay too much. In summer, temperatures can easily reach the 40s, so it's a good season for lounging on the beach or making the most of the air-con found in practically all hotels, restaurants and museums.

## Find out more

**www.btea.bh** – The official site of the Bahrain Tourism and Exhibition Authority. You can also download the very comprehensive app, simply called Bahrain. They also have an Instagram account: www.instagram.com/tourismbh/.
**www.culture.gov.bh** – News and information on cultural highlights and a calendar of upcoming events (in English).
**www.pearlingpath.bh** – A very informative website (available in English) on the Pearling Path in Muharraq.
**www.shaikhebrahimcenter.org** – Lots of information about the buildings renovated in Muharraq and Manama by the foundation along with a calendar of future events.

## What to pack

Lightweight clothes are an absolute must for the hot climate. But do bring additional layers for the cooler winter evenings and to keep warm in hotels, restaurants, museums and other places where the air-con can be chilly. Pack dressier outfits if you're planning on eating out in one of the more fashionable establishments. Keep shorts, swim shorts and more revealing attire for beaches and resorts. In the street, showing too much flesh (this applies to both men and women) is considered somewhat offensive.
At the beach, swimsuits shouldn't be too skimpy.
First-aid kit: bring sun cream and sufficient quantities of any medications you are taking to last you during your trip. Local pharmacies are well stocked with common items.

# Basic information

## Shopping

It's hard to resist the temptation of bringing home a souvenir from Bahrain. There's something for every taste and budget. For each category listed below, find places to shop in the Addresses section.

### Jewellery

In Manama Souq, dozens of windows glisten with gold, pendants, rings and other fineries.Spectacular to behold perhaps, but not always practical to wear. Among them you will find designers with an eye for blending classic forms and contemporary styles. If it's the famous Bahraini pearls you're after, we highly recommend going to a reputable vendor. Some have been in business for over a hundred years.

### Carpets and rugs

Bahrain doesn't weave its own carpets and rugs, although they are part of the local culture. The carpets and rugs you find in Bahrain – available in a wide range of prices – are typically imported from Iran, Afghanistan or Pakistan.

### Textiles

There is a weaving tradition in Bahrain that the authorities are striving to revive. However, you won't find these pieces in Manama Souq (where shoppers prefer Indian and Bangladeshi textiles) but rather in the designer shops in the malls.

### Spices and confectionery

The souqs in Manama and Muharraq have spice shops galore, offering plenty of opportunities to stock up on **bezar**, a traditional Arabian spice blend of cumin, fennel, turmeric and chilli. Mild at first, it packs a spicy punch at the finish. The perfect seasoning for fish. Another classic food to bring home is **halva**, a dessert made from almonds, pistachios and a load of sugar!

### Crafts

Pottery and woodworking are two techniques young Bahraini artisans are bringing into the 21st century. Check out their wares in the 'Made in Bahrain' stores and in **A'Ali**, the country's pottery centre (*p. 56*).

## Alcohol

Drinking is permitted in bars and restaurants with an alcohol licence. This generally means higher-category hotels and restaurants in the swankier parts of town. Local cafés and neighbourhood restaurants don't serve alcohol. Some large supermarkets will have a wine and spirits section.

## Embassies

**U.S. Embassy in Bahrain** – Bldg. 979, Rd 3119, Block 331, Zinj, Manama - *1724 2700* - bh.usembassy.gov.
**Honorary Consulate of Canada**– GFH Tower, 16th Floor, Building 1411, Rd 4626, Block 346, Bahrain Financial Harbour District, Manama - travel.gc.ca.
**British Embassy**– 21 Government Ave, Manama 306 - *1757 4100 -www.gov.uk*.

**Australia**– There is no diplomatic representation of Australia in Bahrain. If needed, Australian citizens can contact the Australian Embassy in Saudi Arabia: Abdullah bin Hozafa Al-Sahmi Ave, Diplomatic Quarter, Riyadh - *966 11 250 0900 - www.dfat.gov.au*.

## Swimming and water sports

The island's crystal-clear waters are a permanent invitation to go for a dip. Many seaside resorts have their own private beach, some of which are open to non-guests (*Addresses p. 90*). Arguably the most stunning public beach is **Al Jazair**, in the south of the island (*p. 65*). Head there if you want to swim or partake in a range of water-based activities. One must-do is the excursion to **Al Jaradah** Island, a patch of golden sand lapped by turquoise waters (*p. 66*).



**Sea Masters diving and sea tours** – *347, B5 Road 59, Amwaj - 973 3383 3388 - sea-masters-scuba-instructor.business.site*. This company organises dives and sea excursions including trips out to Al Jaradah Island.

### Diving

The translucent waters are ideal for putting on your snorkel and fins to explore the ocean wildlife. And why not go on the hunt for oyster pearls while you're down there? Tourist divers are allowed to collect up to 60 oysters from the seabed, so there's a high chance of taking home one or two pearls.
Find a host of water sports options on the Tourism Authority app (*p. 97*), from jet skiing, parasailing and diving to boat hire and even water jet packs.

## Local time

Bahrain is 3 hours ahead of GMT and does not observe daylight saving time. When it's noon in New York, Ottawa or Montreal, it's 8pm in Bahrain in winter and 7pm in summer. When it's noon in London, it's 3pm in Bahrain in winter and 2pm in summer. When it's noon in Canberra or Sydney, it's 4am in Bahrain in winter and 5am in summer.

## Electricity

The standard voltage is 230V. Travellers from the US, Canada and Australia will need an adapter as the sockets take different plugs; those from the UK won't have any problem plugging in their electrical devices.

## Disabled access

The main modern hotels, shopping malls, museums and the airport in Bahrain have been designed with disabled access in mind.

## Opening times

The weekend days in Bahrain are Friday and Saturday. Their Sunday is our Monday!
Banks and administrative offices are generally open Sunday to Thursday, from 8am to 5pm. You can usually find bureaux de change open during the weekend.
Lots of malls and local shops stay open from 9am to 9-10pm, including at the weekend. On Fridays, many local businesses will shut up shop for a prayer break at noon.
Museums have variable closing days (*see the visitor information of each museum in the Visit Bahrain section*).

**Calendar of Islamic festivals**

| | 2024 | 2025 | 2026 | 2027 |
|---|---|---|---|---|
| **Start of Ramadan** | 11 March | 1 March | 18 February | 8 February |
| **Eid al-Fitr** | 9 April | 30 March | 19 March | 9 March |
| **Eid al-Adha** | 17 June | 7 June | 27 May | 17 May |
| **Islamic New Year** | 8 July | 27 June | 17 June | 6 June |
| **Ashura** | 17 July | 6 July | 26 June | 15 June |
| **Prophet Muhammad's birthday** | 16 September | 5 September | 26 August | 15 August |

The buildings restored by the Shaikh Ebrahim Center in Muharraq and Manama are closed Fridays.

## Internet

WiFi is available almost everywhere, in hotels, restaurants, shopping malls and so forth.

## Public holidays

**1 January**: New Year.
**1 May**: International Workers' Day.
**16 and 17 December**: National Day.
Other public holidays change from year to year, depending on the Muslim lunar calendar.
**Eid al-Fitr**: end of Ramadan.
**Eid al-Adha**: Feast of Sacrifice.
**Ashura**: celebrated by Shia Muslims, marking the martyrdom of Imam Hussein, grandson of the Prophet Muhammad.
**Islamic New Year**.
**Mawlid**: birth of the Prophet Muhammad.

## Official language

The official language of Bahrain is Arabic, although its standardised form known as Modern Standard Arabic (MSA) is the mother tongue of only 1% of Bahrainis. MSA is a lingua franca used by Arabic speakers of different dialects to communicate. English, which became widespread during the British protectorate, is extensively used and serves as the bridge language between Bahrainis and the migrant population. Road signs are displayed in Arabic and English.

## Press

The English-language daily, *News of Bahrain* , covers the latest news across the kingdom. It's available at news stands, in the main hotels and online: *www.newsofbahrain.com.*
The monthly magazine, *Bahrain This Month*, contains a comprehensive guide to the events happening that

month and interesting features.
For the digital version go to *www.bahrainthismonth.com*

## Ramadan

During Islam's holy month (*calendar p. 101*), Muslims fast from sunrise to sunset. **Iftar** is the fast-breaking meal Muslims enjoy after sunset, a time for festivities with family, friends and neighbours. All major hotels put on gargantuan buffets for Iftar and a host of events in the evening. Visitors should expect slower activity during the day and abstain from eating, drinking and smoking in public. Hotel restaurants stay open for tourists at lunchtime.

## Healthcare



The standard of care in Bahrain is comparable to that found in the UK or US. Tap water is drinkable and the country has no endemic diseases to speak of.
Medical facilities and hospitals are completely satisfactory.
Be aware that if you are hospitalised for any reason, you will have to settle there and then any medical bills, which can be costly. **Taking out travel insurance before you leave is strongly advised**, and will cover you for hospitalisation and repatriation should you need it. Some credit cards include this type of insurance so check with your bank.
The website of the UK's Foreign, Commonwealth & Development Office provides foreign travel advice with up-to-date information on the health and security situation of every country: *https://www.gov.uk/foreign-travel-advice*

## Safety

Generally speaking, Bahrain is very safe to visit. You should have no trouble walking around the streets, day or night. This includes solo female travellers, provided they are not dressed immodestly by Bahraini standards which, at worst, can attract disapproving looks.

## Taxis

There is no shortage in Manama or Muharraq of taxis, which provide comfortable transportation from one district to another. The use of meters is compulsory in Bahrain: if the driver does not turn it on (a rare occurrence), refuse the ride and get out of the cab. The average fare in Manama: 5 BD ($13). For a longer journey, expect to pay 10 BD/hour ($27). Most drivers speak English. There's a taxi rank with a constant stream of cabs outside Bab Al-Bahrain Souq.
**Bahrain Taxi Group** – *6696 6976 - www.bh-taxigroup.com.*
**Uber** is available in Bahrain.

## Phone

### Calling from abroad

Dial 011 from the US, 11 from Canada or Australia and 00 from the UK followed by 973 (country code) then the number you want to reach.

### Calling from Bahrain

To the US or Canada: dial 00 followed by 1, then the number you want to reach.
To the UK: dial 00 followed by 44, then the number you want to reach.
To Australia: dial 00 followed by 61, then the number you want to reach.

### Mobiles

Your mobile phone should usually connect to the Bahraini network, although charges are likely to be extortionate, including to receive calls and texts.
Ideally, buy a local SIM card when you get there and insert it into your phone (or better still into a second phone). Three operators share the network: **Batelco**, **STC** and **Zain**. They all have outlets at the airport (and in town) where you can purchase a prepaid SIM card, from around $20. You will have to show your passport to make your purchase.
**WhatsApp** is widely used. Most mobile phones are connected to the app.

## Public transport

A wide and punctual network of comfy buses covers the island. It offers a practical way to get between neighbourhoods in the Manama-Muharraq metropolitan area or to reach destinations further out from the capital. However, there are far fewer interregional connections: the network branches out in a star configuration from Manama city centre. Bus fares: 300 fils ($8, purchased on board), a 6-day pass with unlimited journeys costs 7 BD ($18.50, purchased from machines at Manama Bus Terminal or on board). Most routes leave from the Bus Terminal (*detachable map*), a 10-min. walk from Bab Al-Bahrain.
**www.bahrainbus.bh** – This app available in English provides route information from your current location and a real-time bus schedule.

## Sightseeing

### Culture Pass

This ticket gives access to all the 20 or so buildings restored under the aegis of the Shaikh Ebrahim Center. You can only purchase it at the **Shaikh Ebrahim Visitor Center in Muharraq** or the **Manamat Al Gosaibi in Manama** (*p. 18*). It's valid for one day only and costs 3 BD ($8).

### Guided tours

Hiring an official guide is the best way to explore the authentic side of historic Manama and Muharraq. They'll spill the city's secrets and take you into places you wouldn't have otherwise known existed. Find a list of official guides on the **Bahrain Tourism and Exhibition Authority** app and get in touch directly with them via WhatsApp. Also go to *visitbahrain.bh*



## Cars

You can easily get around Manama and Muharraq by hopping between buses, taxis and Ubers. If you're planning on exploring the rest of the island, consider hiring a car. The road network is excellent, Bahraini drivers are pretty disciplined, and there is generally compliance with the highway code. Traffic jams are nonetheless a common occurrence in the city centre at rush hour. Another bonus is that petrol prices are incredibly reasonable: 0.20 BD/l (equivalent to $0.45).Major rental companies have counters at the airport and offices in the city:
**Hertz** - *www.hertz.bh*
**Budget** - *www.budgetbahrain.com*
You might find a good deal on the car hire comparison website *www.rentalcars.com* that offers competitive prices.

# Festivals and events

## Annual events

### Period of Ramadan

▶ **Bahrain Heritage Festival** – This five-day festival during Ramadan honours the kingdom's cultural traditions with a programme of music, crafts, Ramadan dishes and folk games. Al Baradah Souq, Muharraq. www.culture.gov.bh

### Mid-February to mid-April

▶ **Spring of Culture** – This annual festival packs in events, concerts, exhibitions, folk music and culinary events (**Muharraq Supper Club**) at various locations. Find the programme at springofculture.org



### March

▶ **Bahrain International Garden Show** – Over three days in March. The leading gardening and agriculture show in the Arabian Gulf. Every year, this event draws almost 50,000 visitors to Sakhir's Exhibition World Bahrain.
www.bigs.com.bh

▶ **Bahrain Food Festival** – The biggest food festival in the Arabian Gulf. Over 100 restaurants take part in this annual event, a great opportunity to discover an abundance of cuisines, especially local.

▶ **Formula One Grand Prix** – Usually in March unless it falls during Ramadan. Bahrain International Circuit in Sakhir attracts an enthusiastic crowd for its Grand Prix, transforming this race meeting into a great show of national pride. You don't have to be a petrolhead to enjoy this annual F1 event. www.bahraingp.com

### May-June

▶ **Bahrain Annual Fine Arts Exhibition** – This exhibition showcases works by the country's home-grown and resident artistic talents. Bahrain National Theatre. www.culture.gov.bh

### July

▶ **Bahrain Summer Festival** – Aimed at a young audience (ages 7-15), this programme of activities, workshops and live performances takes place all over Manama.

### October

▶ **Bahrain International Music Festival** – Over five days, Manama welcomes folk bands and musicians from the Arab world and beyond. Concerts are hosted at the Culture Hall, close to the National Theatre. www.culture.gov.bh

### December

▶ **Muharraq Nights** – Over two weekends, Muharraq comes to life with concerts, exhibitions, poetry readings, open-air markets, arts and crafts and much more. Highlights include folk singing by local pearl fishers at the Dar Al Muharraq (*p. 31*).
www.pearlingpath.bh

To find out about current and upcoming events, go to www.calendar.bh/en

Bahrain International Garden Show

dough

# FIND OUT MORE





A stroll around hypermodern Bahrain Bay.
©Eric Sander (ericsander.com)

# Key dates in Bahrain's history

**Ca. 6000 BC** – Around this time, the island starts to break away from the Arabian Continent.
**5000 - 4000 BC** – First human occupation identified by excavations of shards of pottery from Mesopotamia, evidence of trading.
**3300 BC** – First mention of the country named Dilmun on a clay tablet found in Uruk, south of present-day Iraq.
**2300 - 2050 BC** – Appearance of the first fields of tumuli.
**2050 - 1650 BC** – Dilmun forms an independent kingdom and becomes the nexus of maritime trade between Mesopotamia, Oman and the Indus Valley. Its capital is Qal'at Al Bahrain port.
Monarchs are buried in the royal graveyard in A'ali.
**2100 BC** – Construction of the first Barbar Temple.
**2150 - 1400 BC**– *The Epic of Gilgamesh*, the earliest known work of literature, is the story of the voyage of Sumerian king Gilgamesh who dives into the Dilmun Sea to salvage the flower of immortality, believed to be a pearl.
**1650 - 1000 BC** – Babylon, under the rule of the Kassite dynasty, takes control of Bahrain. The Kassite government installs its seat in Qal'at Al Bahrain and rebuilds the city, including large trade warehouses.
**1000 - 400 BC** – Dilmun switches to Assyrian rule and the city of Qal'at Al Bahrain is rebuilt once again.



**544 BC** – Last mention of Dilmun, found inscribed on a clay tablet.
**325 BC** – Alexander the Great returns from India and orders the exploration of the Gulf's Arabian shore. A Greek expedition reaches Bahrain. For a time, Bahrain is known as Tylos, its Greek name which was used until the 2nd century AD. The archipelago becomes part of the Seleucid Empire following the conquests of Alexander the Great.
**129 AD** – Bahrain falls under the rule of the Parthians then the Sasanians after the latter defeated the former in Iran.
**200** – Arab tribes dominate Bahrain.
**629 -900** – The message from Prophet Muhammad reaches Bahrain and many Arabs and Persians convert to Islam. At this time, Bahrain is a cosmopolitan society including Jewish, Christian and Zoroastrian communities.
**692 - 1000** – Al Khamis Mosque is founded in 692. An inscription discovered on the site suggests however a more recent date (11th c.).
**900 - 1077** – Bahrain falls under the rule of the Qarmatis, a Shia Ismaili group from Eastern Arabia who revolted against the Abbasid Caliphate. They attack pilgrims on the way to Mecca, which they pillage in 930, stealing and holding to ransom the Black Stone from the Kaaba. They are defeated in 1076, ending their domination over Bahrain.

**1077 - 1520** – The Qarmatis are overturned by the Uyunid dynasty, originating from Bahrain and allies of the Seljuks from Iran. Their capital, Qatif (Saudi Arabia), is moved to Awal (Bahrain). Under their rule, the state extends as far as Kuwait.
**1520 - 1602** – After conquering Ormuz, the Portuguese set their sights on Bahrain, which they colonise from 1521. Struggle of influence with the Ottomans for control of the region.
**1602 - 1620** – Weakened by their fight against the Ottomans and other emerging European powers, the Portuguese are driven out by the Bahrainis with Persian assistance.
**1620 - 1737** – Bahrain becomes part of the Persian Empire.
**1737 - 1783** – Bahrain falls under Omani domination.
**1811** – After an initial invasion of Bahrain in the early 1780s, the Al Khalifa family seizes definitive control of the archipelago in 1811.
**1820** – A treaty is signed between Great Britain and Bahrain, which becomes a British protectorate.
**1911** – French jeweller Jacques Cartier makes his first pearl-buying trip.
**1919** – Bahrain becomes the first Gulf country to establish a public school for boys, open to girls from 1928.
**1924** – A Royal Air Force plane makes its first landing in Bahrain, signalling the creation of the first airport in the Gulf region.
**1930** – The arrival of Japanese-farmed pearls sends the Bahraini pearl market into free fall.
**1931** – Albert Londres publishes his report, *Pearl fishers*.
**1932** – Bahrain becomes the first country in the Gulf to extract oil.
**1970** – The emir Sheikh Isa bin Salman Al Khalifa decides that his country will not join the federation which would unite Bahrain, Qatar and the United Arab Emirates.
**1971** – Bahrain proclaims its independence.
**1976** – Concorde makes it first commercial flight: London-Bahrain.
**1979** – Ayatollah Khomeini's rise to power in Iran ignites political tensions in Bahrain where its Shia community is directly concerned by the Islamic Revolution.
**2001** – A national charter is ratified in a referendum by 98.4% of voters.
**2002** – Bahrain changes from an absolute monarchy to a constitutional monarchy.
**2004** – The international F1 circuit in Sakhir opens.
**2009** – Bahrain is the first Gulf state to abandon 'kafala', a sponsorship system for migrant labourers, allowing them to change jobs without their employer's agreement.
**2020** – The Abraham Accords are signed, normalising diplomatic relations between Israel and Bahrain. Manama synagogue is opened after being closed for over 75 years.
**2021** – Our Lady of Arabia Cathedral is opened.
**2022** – Pastoral visit of Pope Francis to Bahrain.

# One of the world's earliest civilisations.

## The Dilmun civilisation in the Bronze Age

The history of Bahrain is closely intertwined with the Dilmun civilisation, which flourished in the Arabian Gulf during the Bronze Age, between 2500 and 1800 BC. The site of **Qal'at Al Bahrain**, added to Unesco's World Heritage List in 2005, was the former capital of Dilmun. At that time, Bahrain was a strategic nexus of a trade network between the Arabian Peninsula, the Indus Valley and Oman. Timber, copper, fish, precious stones, pearls and pottery were some of the many types of cargo shipped along these routes. Evidence of the region's commercial success, the thousands of tumuli in Bahrain – large artificial mounds built to cover graves – make the archipelago the largest prehistoric cemetery in the world.



Sumerian texts from the period are full of references to Dilmun's prosperity. Dilmun is even the setting of the saga of Enki and Ninhursag, central to the Sumerian creation myth. The Dilmun pearl is said to have the power to give eternal life in the story of **Gilgamesh**, part man, part god, who legend has it placed the pearl in the mouth of a sea serpent.

When the Indus Valley Civilisation collapsed around 1800 BC and Bahrain lost its role as a trade port, the country had to wait another 400 years before it reclaimed its strategic place in the Arabian Gulf, achieved thanks to the Kassites, a Mesopotamian dynasty, who settled there around 1450 BC. The Kassites planted a Babylonian colony in Bahrain, securing its control of the maritime trade routes. But Bahrain's return to significance was short lived. Weakened by the Assyrian invasion of Babylon led by King Tukulti-Ninurta I in 1225 BC, the Kassites never recovered. Bahrain was brought under Babylonian rule, and there was no further mention of the Dilmun civilisation in texts from that period for hundreds of years.

## Bahrain and the Seleucid Empire

There's scant information about Bahrain for the period between the 4th century BC and the 7th century AD. We do know that the archipelago maintained strong ties with the Kingdom of Characene, as a port for trade, since the islands fell under the control of the Parthians and the Sasanians whose empire reached its apogee in 610 AD. We can also state with some certainty that Bahrain was in regular contact with the Seleucid Empire during this time.

A mint was established on the island, producing silver tetradrachms struck for Alexander the Great. Various objects bearing Greek inscriptions and dated around the 4th c. BC have also been unearthed in Bahrain. These finds seem to support the theory that the Seleucids, a dynasty descended from Seleucus (358-281 BC), a general under Alexander the Great, were in control of Bahrain at some point. This theory continues nonetheless to be a regular subject of historical debate. The name 'Dilmun' associated with Bahrain was later changed to the Greek name **Tylos**, attributed to the main island of the archipelago following the expedition led by Nearchus, a navarch (admiral) under Alexander the Great around 325 AD. After the successful Indian campaign of **Alexander the Great** , it is believed his ambitions turned to conquering the Arabian Peninsula.

We know too that the archipelago flourished during this period when its cultural development was strongly driven by Hellenistic culture. Tylos was said to harbour a wealth of flora, according to Androsthenes, who led an expedition there, his botanical data later used by Theoprastus. Pliny the Elder also included an inventory of the island's plantlife in his *Naturalis Historia*, published in 77 AD: a mangrove (now almost gone), cotton fields and a wide variety of fruit, date and fig trees and vines. The abundance of underground freshwater resources in Bahrain no doubt accounted in no small part for this cornucopia. Furthermore, Greek scholar Ptolemy mentions Tylos in his *Geographia*,

Nearly 12,000 tumuli have survived from the Dilmun era.

written around 150 AD, as does Greek geographer Isidore of Charax who describes pearl fishing in Bahrain.

## A land of Islam

After living under the domination of tribes from Yemen and Hejaz, the archipelago fell under the rule of the Sasanians, a dynasty founded by Ardashir, the governor of the Achaemenid province of Fars, who appointed his son, Shapur, governor of Bahrain. In the 6th century, the Persian Empire appointed a marshal to govern Bahrain, which henceforth served as a naval base. It was during this time that the capital of Bahrain was renamed Shirin, doubtless in homage to the name of a wife of Khosrow II, the last great Sasanian king. In some texts, her name is spelled 'Dirin'.



Islam quickly assumed a fundamental place in Bahrain. In the 7th c., most people in the region were polytheist, despite the presence of small Christian and Jewish communities. It is thought that Christianity had spread to Bahrain several centuries earlier from Persian Chaldea. In 629, seven years after the start of the Arabian conquest, King Al Munzir ibn Sawa Al Tamimi, a member of the Arab dynasty that ruled the archipelago, embraced Islam. Like other rulers, he would have received a letter from the Prophet **Muhammad** himself, asking him to convert. From then on, Islam, and the use of Arabic, spread across the country. One of the first mosques in the Arabian Gulf was built in Bahrain, in 692: **Al Khamis Mosque**, one of the oldest mosques in the world. An inscription discovered at the site suggests however that it's actually more recent than originally thought, probably dating from the 11th century.

Philippe Orain/Michelin

This statuette at the Bahrain National Museum is evidence of trade with the Greek-Roman world.

The overthrow by the Abbasids of the Umayyad dynasty, who controlled the Muslim world until 750 AD, coincided with a geopolitical shift in the region, marking the beginning of the Islamic Golden Age. Bahrain entered a prosperous period which lasted until the end of the Abbasid Caliphate, around 1250, reclaiming its strategic port position for the transit of imported goods, mostly coming from Asia.

The Arabian cultural and intellectual world flourished thanks to the ensuing commercial exchanges and countless expeditions. Voyages strengthened knowledge of the sea, in particular the Indian Ocean, the western coast of

India and the Red Sea. Many scholars emerged in this period, with the likes of Sheikh Maitham Al Bahrani, and became prominent for their knowledge of geography, astronomy and theology.
The Qarmati revolution from the 10th c. once again destabilised the political balance in Bahrain and its region. The Qarmatis were a militant Shia Ismaili movement, today considered heretics. Abu-Sa'd Al Jannabi was sent by the Qarmatis to Bahrain where he established a form of republic based on reason and equality in which the government consisted of six scholars and properties were shared with the Qarmatis. During the Sack of Mecca in January 930, the Black Stone in the Kaaba was sent to Al Hajar (in present-day Bahrain) by the Qarmatis. The Abbasids finally overthrew the Qarmatis in the late 11th c. and took control of the region, which stayed under Sunni rule until the 15th c., and notably the domination of the Uyunids from the 11th to the 13th c., before the arrival of the Omanis in Bahrain in 1483.

## From Portuguese to Persian

By the late 14th c., Portuguese navigators had gained control of large swathes of the coast of West Africa. But they had yet to find the maritime route that would take them to India and further expand their foothold in Asia. The Arabian Gulf regained importance as a strategic point of passage that the Ottoman and Portuguese empires vied to control. Bahrain was explored by Portuguese navigator Duarte Barbosa in 1485, then invaded by the Portuguese army in 1521, placing the archipelago under Portuguese rule for 80 years. The struggle for influence between the Ottomans and the Portuguese showed no signs of letting up, and culminated in 1559 when the Ottoman governor Al Hasa waged a campaign to seize the island via the port of Qatif. Seventy-three ships were chartered and 800 men led the siege of Manama on 2 July 1559. The commander of the Portuguese army, based in Ormuz, sent reinforcements to the 400 soldiers, mostly Persian, tasked with defending the island.
Out of provisions and munitions, the Ottomans took refuge in a palm grove. They finally surrendered and were forced to relinquish their weapons and horses to the enemy and pay a fine of one million akçe.
The sizeable Shia community in Bahrain, despite the royal family being Sunni, dates back to the 17th c. The Persians took control of the archipelago from 1601 onwards under the leadership of the shah of Iran, Abbas I. The Portuguese occupiers, their position sorely weakened by its long conflict with the Ottoman Empire and the emergence of other European powers, were chased out by the Bahrainis during a popular uprising. Bahrain was now under the jurisdiction of Beglarbegi of Kuhgilu whose seat was in Behbahan, Iran. The Safavids, one of the greatest Muslim powers of the era along with the Ottoman Empire and the Mughal Empire, ruled Bahrain until 1717. A Shia intellectual elite began to form in the country, its members including Yusuf Al Bahrani (1695-1772), and Safavid ideology spread until the empire collapsed, weakened by an

An ancient parchment from the wonderful collections at the Beit Al Qur'an (House of the Quran).

invasion from Afghanistan in the early 18th c. Oman took control of Bahrain in 1717, starting a new chapter in the country's political history. Despite the Persians' defeat, it's interesting to point out that Iranian claims over Bahrain have never really ceased to this day, including in recent times. **Ayatollah Khomeini**'s rise to power in Iran, from 1979, sparked, amongst other things, new political tensions in Bahrain, where its Shia community was directly concerned by the Islamic Revolution. An attempted Iranian coup designed to seize control of Bahrain was uncovered in Manama in 1981. The plotters were suspected of being trained in Iran to overthrow the Bahraini regime. Relations between the two countries nevertheless improved following the visit of King Fahd of Saudi Arabia to Iran in 2002.

# Sovereignty challenged by the protectorate

## The House of Khalifa seeks power over Bahrain

The first successful conquest of Bahrain by the Al Khalifa family was led in 1783 by Sheikh Ahmed bin Muhammad Al Khalifa, commonly referred to as Ahmed al-Fateh (Ahmed the Conqueror) (1725-1795). The Sunni Al Khalifa family belong to the Anizah tribe, which was based in Kuwait and so was able to rely on Kuwait's naval fleet and an alliance with the Bedouin clans. In 1799, however, the House of Khalifa was overthrown by a coalition between the Omanis and the House of Saud who appointed the Sultan of Oman and then the Wahhabis as the rulers of Bahrain. The Al Khalifa family launched a second invasion of Bahrain in 1811, aided by long-standing Sunni Bedouin Arab dynasties including the Al Benali, Al Galahma and Al Dossari clans. The Al Khalifa family took control of Bahrain for the second time and have maintained it ever since.

The British Empire, which held a strong influence over the Arabian Gulf in this period, officially recognised the Al Khalifa family's domination of the archipelago in a treaty signed in 1820. Under its terms, the Al Khalifa family committed not to engage in any act of piracy except during times of war. In 1830, the Ottoman Empire regained control of the Arabian Peninsula through Muhammad Ali Pasha (1769-1849), the ruler of Egypt. The Al Khalifa family then decided to swear allegiance to the Iranians to protect themselves from attack, then to the British, in 1861, in the Perpetual Truce of Peace and Friendship signed by Sheikh Muhammad bin Khalifa and Colonel Lewis Pelly (1825-1892). Twice-renewed, in 1892 and 1951, this treaty guaranteed Bahrain the support of the British Empire in the event of attack, and renewed the Al Khalifa family's rule of the country.



## The British protectorate

Rather than speak of colonising Bahrain, the British Empire preferred to refer to it as a 'State protected by the British' or an 'independent State under British protection'. The Al Khalifa family's domestic sovereignty was restated several times by the British, such as in 1927 during a new episode of Persian claims to Bahraini rule: 'The accords [between Great Britain and Bahrain since 1820] have all agreed that the Sheikh of Bahrain is an independent sovereign.' During this period, however, Britain maintained control of Bahrain's foreign relations and had right of veto over certain diplomatic relationships.

At the same time, Bahrain stood out from other powers in the Arabian Gulf in the way its citizens lived and how society was organised, under

Persian and Indian influence. Several wealthy merchant families on the island in the 19th c. were Persian. Bahrain's close proximity to the Indian subcontinent also had an important impact on Bahraini culture, fashion and education. Despite the huge disparity between Bahrain's inhabitants - locals, foreigners and colonists -, harmony already existed in the country, which was modernised under the authority of Isa bin Ali Al Khalifa (1848-1932), who came to power in 1869. The economy was shaping into a modern economy. Relations also improved between the Al Khalifa families in Qatar and in Bahrain, in the grip of strong tensions until then. From 1870, Bahrain became an important trading hub for the Arabian Gulf region, ahead of Basra, Muscat and Kuwait.

D.R.

In 1905, there were 15,000 divers, mostly based on the island of Muharraq.

# Towards independence and modernity

## The pearling trade

Bahrain has been known for its magnificent pearls for millennia. From Sumerian texts to those of the Renaissance and the modern era, it is clear that Bahraini pearls have always been coveted by merchants and seamen. In 1905, there were 15,000 divers out of a population of 99,000 inhabitants, mostly based on the island of Muharraq. World-famous jewellers in the 20th c., including **Jacques Cartier** (1884-1942), heir to the French family of the same name, sourced pearls from Bahrain exclusively from 1912, testifying to the quality of these gems.

## The modern Middle East

Pearl fishing (the pearls caught were exported primarily to India and Europe) was not taxed by the Bahraini government, but the increased purchasing power of its citizens pushed up the consumption of imported products and with it the gross national income. Its coffers full, Bahrain launched a massive investment plan in public services, creating its police force in 1896; its first hospital, in Manama, in 1900, followed by a second one, the American Mission Hospital, in 1902, when the country suffered a serious smallpox epidemic. Bahrain was the first country in the Gulf region to install telegraphy, in 1918, then telephones, in 1932. The archipelago welcomed its first cars, then electricity in Manama and Muharraq, in the 1920s. Important cultural and educational developments were also happening in Bahrain during this period with the opening of the first boys' school (1919) and then girls' school (1928), the first cinema in 1938 and a local radio station in 1940. Bahrain's strategic position was also

### 'The Pearl Fishers' by Albert Londres (1931)

The fascination for Bahrain and its pearls is no better expressed than by the French journalist Albert Londres (1884-1932) in his 1931 report on the country's pearl fishers: 'It's magnificent. If the drinking water were not salty, I'd make my home here. The sea is turquoise, transparent. If I look closely, I'm certain that I'd see oysters agape on the seabed. I'd only have to stick an arm in to grasp a pearl [...] Do you know what is happening in the Arabian Gulf? A despicable thing. More than twenty-five sources of freshwater gush into the sea. While the people, on land, have nothing but salty water to drink, the oysters, on their sandbanks, are gulping down freshwater! And that's what, they say, gives Bahraini pearls their beautiful lustre.'

D.R.

Bahrain was the first country in the Gulf to have a postal service, telegraphy and the telephone.

bolstered by improved access to the country. An airfield was built especially to allow the landing of an RAF plane, on 8 June 1924, flying from its air base in Shaibah, Iraq. A flight path was opened over the country in 1932. This meant that British passengers no longer had to fly over southern Iran, where Russian troops were stationed. The first commercial airline established in Bahrain was operated by the Gulf Aviation Company, now **Gulf Air**, in 1948. While in 1950 Muharraq airport received about 20 passengers a day, today several million passengers pass through every year. After seeing its economy flourish for the first decades of the 20th c., Bahrain was faced with a declining pearling industry with the arrival of Japanese cultured pearls on the market and the Great Depression of the 1930s, almost immediately compensated by the discovery of major onshore oil reserves.

## Independence

Fortified by a century of modernisation and progress, Bahrain proclaimed its independence on **14 August 1971**, refusing to join the Emirati federation supported by the British which would have united Bahrain, Qatar and the United Arab Emirates (UAE). Instead, Bahrain signed a new truce with Great

### Cartier and the pearl trade

Jacques Cartier first came to Bahrain in 1912. At the time, the third son of Louis-François Cartier, who established the famed jewellery company, was running the London store. He supplied the diamond scroll tiara for the coronation of King Edward VII, who dubbed him 'the king of jewellers and the jeweller of kings'. Jacques had just returned from a long tour of Asia in search of exceptional sapphires, rubies and emeralds. But at that time the most coveted gemstone was the pearl, comparable to the diamond today. He travelled to Bahrain to source pearls directly for the family business. After negotiating with the local traders, he struck a deal. Until Japanese cultured pearls arrived on the market, the pearling trade was an important source of income for the Cartier house.

Archive photo of pearl fishers

Courtesy of the Cartier family (Francesca Cartier Brickell)



Archive photo of Jacques Cartier.

Britain in addition to joining the Arab League and the United Nations. The first parliamentary elections were held in 1972, before the Emir of Bahrain, **Sheikh Isa bin Salman Al Khalifa** (1933-1999), dissolved its national assembly in 1975. His son **Hamad bin Isa Al Khalifa** succeeded him in 1999 and changed Bahrain from the status of Emirate (absolute monarchy) to a **constitutional monarchy**.
A two-chamber system (upper house: *shura*/lower house: *nuwab*) was instated after the **national charter** was ratified by referendum in **2001**, with parliamentary elections taking place in 2022, when 147 candidates including eight women contested the 40 seats in the lower chamber. Bahrain was also the first Arab country to abolish the *kafala* system – which required migrant workers to be sponsored – and continued on its path towards democracy by recognising workers' right to strike and freedom of association.

# Bahrain in the Oil Age

**Bahrain was the first country in the Gulf to produce oil.**

In 1908, John Gordon Lorimer, a British journalist and diplomat, reported on indicators of the presence of oil in Bahrain, observing 'a small quantity of bitumen southeast of Jabal Al Dukhan' in Pliocene rock, a theory corroborated later by a team sent to the site by Admiral Edmund Slade. But it wasn't until 1932 that the first concession was granted to New Zealander Frank Holmes, later to be sold on to the American Eastern Gulf Oil Company then the Standard Oil Company of California. The Bahrain Petroleum Company (known today as **BAPCO**), officially set up in 1929, discovered huge quantities of oil south of Mount Jabal Al Dukhan on 2 June 1932. BAPCO's rate of production rapidly increased, from 400 barrels a day to 640,000 tonnes of oil in 1936, thanks to exports which started in 1934. By the late 1930s, over a million tonnes of oil in Bahrain was earmarked every year specifically for export. Two refineries were built on Sitra Island in 1936, allowing Bahrain to up its revenue from refining crude oil. Some 25,000 barrels left the Sitra refineries daily, rising to 33,000 during the Second World War, which sent international demand through the roof. The waning pearling industry had scarcely any effect on the Bahraini economy. Bahrain's income skyrocketed thanks to oil, and the country's authorities launched various projects to modernise the country, following the **'three thirds' policy**: one third of oil profit was reinvested in the industry; a second third was invested in social programmes, with the third portion going towards the country's public expenditure. The appetite for oil of neighbouring powers caused a number of border disputes, Bahrain banging heads in particular with Saudi Arabia and Qatar. While the conflict with Saudi Arabia was settled in 1951, the dispute with Qatar, relating to the Hawar Islands, lasted until 2001, resolved by the UN International Court of Justice, in favour of Bahrain. Projects paid for with oil income included a pipeline between Sitra and Zallaq, than another terminating in Saudi Arabia. Access to electricity and water, until then reserved for the cities, was extended to the whole country. But the greatest innovation of the age was undoubtedly the swing bridge connecting the country's two main cities, Muharraq and Manama, built in 1942, which was enthusiastically received by the Bahrainis. Other links were soon constructed to facilitate trade and movement between the islands in the archipelago, such as the bridge between Sitra Island and the main island of Bahrain, and the **King Fahd Causeway**, a 15.5-mile-long bridge connecting Bahrain with Saudi Arabia, named after Fahd bin Abdulaziz Al Saud (1921-2005), ruler of Saudi Arabia from 1982 to 2005

(p. 55). Extensive urban development programmes radically changed the country: out went the traditional barasti, traditional huts made from clay and palm fronds, and in came brand new public buildings that completely transformed Manama's seafront. A ceremonial gateway was also erected in Manama in 1945: **Bab Al Bahrain**, the site of Sheikh Salman bin Hamad's new offices. Bahrain's pioneering spirit in the field of urbanisation is alive and well today, yet the country has managed to preserve among the frenetic real estate development some vestiges of its prosperous past, such as the traditional Manama Souq, the customs offices, and the old Court of Justice.



## A diversified economy

The first Gulf country to anticipate the growing scarcity of its oil resources, Bahrain resolved to diversify its industrial activity from the 1960s through aluminium, of which the country is now one of the world's biggest producers. Aluminium Bahrain (**ALBA**) was founded in 1971 with the aim of reducing the country's oil dependence by investing in a profitable commodity. From 120,000 tonnes of aluminium produced in 1971 to over 1.5 million tonnes in 2022, the company now employs 3,100 people, 84% of whom are Bahraini. ALBA sells 45% of its production locally with the rest exported to other parts of the Middle East and to Europe, Africa and North America.

An ancient trade hub, Bahrain is a country that has stayed true to its commercial heritage. Several major corporations were established in the 20th c., such as **Batelco**, which has developed telecommunications networks across the Gulf, as well as family-owned firms, like **The Kanoo Group**, one of the premier conglomerates in the Middle East, with interests in shipping, petrochemicals, tourism, real estate, finance and information technology.

Bahrain has also pumped investment into the petrochemical industry, setting up **GPIC**, a joint venture between its government and the PIC (Kuwaiti) and SABIC (Saudi) companies. GPIC began its activity in Bahrain by producing 1,100 tonnes a day of ammonia and methanol, back in 1985. Current production totals 1.6 million tonnes of urea, ammonia and methanol at three plants on a 600,000-sq.m site. Expert forecasts on Bahrain's onshore reserves are very positive. GPIC has its own water desalination and demineralisation facilities. The company employs mostly Bahrainis, 14% of whom are women.

Oil and gas only accounts for 10% of Bahrain's GDP.



Importantly, in the 1980s Bahrain became a major financial centre when, during the Lebanon War (1975-1990), Middle Eastern banks relocated their regional offices from Beirut to Manama. Bahrain's offshore status further enhanced its appeal, promoting the repatriation of capital belonging to Arab investors following the attacks on the World Trade Center in New York on 11 September 2001. Bahraini bank assets currently total 600% of GDP, or 206 billion dollars. Financial services are the second-biggest sector in Bahrain's economy. Most of these companies are concentrated in **Financial Harbour**, Manama's ultramodern financial district, home to 400 financial institutions and a rising number of operators in Islamic finance (banned from investing in sectors considered unlawful under Sharia law, e.g. alcohol, tobacco, gambling), a rapidly growing sector.

# Bahrain in the 21st century

## The smallest Arab country

Bordered by Iran, Saudi Arabia and Qatar, Bahrain is composed of thirty or so flat limestone islands covering a surface area of just over 293 sq.mi, making the archipelago the smallest of the Arab countries. The most populated islands are the island of Bahrain, where the capital Manama is located, and the island of Muharraq, home to the international airport. In the west, **Umm an Nasan Island**, the kingdom's fourth-largest island by size, is a natural sanctuary for wildlife. In the east, the **island of Sitra** is Bahrain's industrial centre. The southern **Hawar Islands** lie close to the maritime boundary with Qatar. One-third of Bahrain's islands are uninhabited, and it is estimated that 10% of Bahrain's land mass has been reclaimed from the sea.



Bahrain may be a small country, but it's prosperous and well developed thanks to its range of buoyant industries (notably gas, oil, aluminium) and the boom in financial services. A Bahraini sovereign fund (Mumtalakat) was established for non-oil assets, in 2006. It manages a portfolio estimated at 17.5 billion dollars in 2022. The country's GDP per capita (PPP) was over 45,000 dollars in 2021 and life expectancy 77 years.

Bahrain has a population of 1.7 million, half of whom are migrant workers, mostly originating from India, Pakistan, Iran and the Philippines. While Arabic is the kingdom's official language, you'll frequently hear other tongues on the island, including Urdu, Farsi and English, the latter being spoken by most Bahrainis. The subtropical climate is arid but the fauna is abundant. Hawar Island is, for example, a sanctuary for migratory birds, where over 350 species have been logged. The presence of freshwater sources in the country for millennia is probably one of the reasons for this, even if current reserves are drying up. The kingdom's name comes from the dual form of the Arabic word *bahr* (sea) – 'al-Bahrayn' literally meaning 'the two seas' – and alludes to the freshwater sources that mingle with the salt waters of Bahrain.

## A constitutional and democratic monarchy

After a brief parliamentary experiment from 1972 to 1975, Bahrain officially switched from the status of emirate to constitutional monarchy in 2002. In 2001, a **National Charter** was approved by 98.4 % of voters in a referendum. On top of the general elections held regularly since 2002, a package of democratic reforms was unveiled by **King Hamad bin Isa Al Khalifa**, most notably the setting up of the Bahrain Tender Board to ensure transparent and fair access to public tenders, the recognition of various freedoms (of religion and association, for example), and the workers' right to strike. **Hillary Clinton**, when she was US Secretary of State, wrote about

The World Trade Center, a tour de force designed by Shaun Killa, a South African architect based in Dubai.

©Eric Sander (ericsander.com)



The National Charter Monument commemorates the approval by referendum of the National Charter which instituted a parliamentary monarchy.

the kingdom's democratic transition: 'Bahrain has demonstrated that multi-ethnic, multi-confessional societies can address the challenges of their development through peaceful reform and representative institutions.'
In 2022, the UN praised Bahrain's efforts in the areas of public health, education and social welfare (accounting for over 35% of public expenditure) and the fact that Bahraini law does not discriminate between individuals on the basis of gender, race, nationality or skin colour.
Following Bahrain's submission of its first report under the UN International Covenant on Economic, Social and Cultural Rights, the UN did however express concerns regarding the rights of migrant workers in Bahrain.

## Education for all

Free and available to all children up to secondary school age, education has always been a key priority for Bahrain. During the Islamic Golden Age, Bahrain became home to many scholars and theologians, building the country's reputation for intellectual brilliance that exists to this day. In 1919, Bahrain became the first country in the Arabian Gulf to open public schools for boys, followed by girls' schools in 1928. School is compulsory for all children between the ages of 6 and 14. Literacy is over 95% among the 15-24 age group.
In 1986, the country opened its first university, the **University of Bahrain**,

with its largest campus located in Sakhir. It has two other campuses, in Isa Town and Manama. The university has a student population of 22,000 in disciplines including medicine, law, the arts, business management and engineering. It consists of 10 colleges inspired by the Western model. The Bahraini government invests hugely in university programmes, to the annual tune of 110 million dollars. The provision of excellent higher education is an intentional strategy designed to retain Bahraini students who might otherwise be tempted to pursue their studies abroad. The investment appears to be working, given that every year Bahrain is highly ranked among the universities in the Arab world (33rd place in the 2023 QS World University Rankings). Bahrain's national education investment plan, announced in 2005, ushered in a new polytechnic college, an education and training quality authority, and a teacher training college.

D.R.

The University of Bahrain's ultramodern campus.

## Bahraini women's rights

Regarded as one of the most 'liberal' nations in the Gulf region, Bahrain is a pioneer in the recognition of women's rights in the Middle East. In 2002, King Sheikh Hamad bin Isa Al Khalifa appointed six women, including one of Christian faith, to the upper chamber. Other female figures followed hot on the heels of these women members of parliament. Dr. Nada Haffadh was appointed Minister of Health in 2004; Alees Samaan became in 2005 the first woman to chair a parliamentary commission in the Arab world; Houda Nonoo is the first Jewish woman ambassador from an Arab country in the Middle East, serving as Bahraini Ambassador to the US from 2008 to 2013. Minister of Culture between 2010 and 2014, Sheikha Mai bint Mohammed Al Khalifa, a member of the royal family, kick-started the restoration of a major tranche of Bahraini heritage. This came in the form of the creation of the Supreme Council for Women in 2001, to promote the status of Bahraini women and encourage women to take up important roles in their country's development, and heralding the launch of progressive reforms in favour of women's rights. The Council's secretary general Lulwa Al Awahdi is the first woman appointed to a ministerial rank in a GCC (Gulf

Bahrain Football Association

Bahrain's national women's football team, a powerful symbol of Bahraini women's freedoms.

Cooperation Council) member country. Bahraini women today have rights still not granted in other Middle Eastern countries: they can vote, drive, travel unaccompanied and hold a bank account. A far cry from the stereotypes we tend to associate with the Middle East, 75% of Bahraini women over the age of 25 are university graduates, and half of them have jobs, mostly in the kingdom's financial services industry. The international community has often commended the country's proactive policy in favour of women's rights. Indeed, four Bahraini women were nominees for the Nobel Peace Prize in 2007. In 2009, the UN Development Programme ranked Bahrain fourth out of 155 countries for its efforts to improve women's rights.

# Religious harmony

## Islam, the official religion

Islam is the official religion of Bahrain, a country which forged close links with the Muslim religion in its infancy. **Some 99% of Bahrainis are Muslim**, a proportion that drops to 70% if the migrant population is counted. Bahrain's constitution provides for freedom of religion and promotes harmony with other faiths practised in the kingdom: Hinduism, Sikhism, Christianity and Judaism. There's huge diversity even within Bahrain's Muslim community, with Sunni Huwala Arabs coexisting alongside the Shia Baharna and Sunni Maliki Arabs (the group to which the Al Khalifa ruling family belongs), Shia and Sunni Iranians, the Sunni Baloch community and Arab migrants, the majority being Sunni. The kingdom's first Islamic public school opened in 1943. Bahrain also opened a museum dedicated to Islam in 1990. **Beit Al Qur'an** *(p. 26)* accommodates one of the finest collections of original Qurans in the world, most sourced from the personal collection of the museum's owner Abdul Latif Jassim Kanoo. Major works in the collection include the first Latin translation dating from 955 AD and the first printed edition of the Quran, from 1664.

## Religious diversity

Christian presence in Bahrain dates from the early centuries AD. The first Christian mission came to the island in 1896. The **current Christian community – 14% of the country's population** – is predominantly Filipino. They congregate for major events at the **Cathedral of Our Lady of Arabia** *(p. 60)*, the biggest cathedral in the Middle East, visited by **Pope Francis** in November 2022.

A large number of migrant workers from the Indian subcontinent are Sikh or Hindu. There is, indeed, a **Hindu temple** *(p. 17)* in Bab Al Bahrain, the historic centre of Manama, within the 'Little India' development, funded by the Bahraini government.

Lastly, Bahrain has the **largest Jewish community of all the Arab countries in the Gulf**, and an Israeli embassy since 2021.

# Lifestyle

## Bahraini hospitality: second nature

Akin to most countries in the Gulf, Bahraini society is incredibly cosmopolitan. However, although foreigners account for about half of Bahrain's population, you won't have any trouble meeting actual Bahrainis, which contrasts, for example, with the Emirates, where the native citizens tend to keep themselves to themselves.

Bahrainis have a reputation for being friendly and open, as is often true of islanders with a trading heritage.

At the crossroads of trade routes between Mesopotamia and India, Bahrain was an essential place to stop and stock up on freshwater and do business. The country's amazing hospitality and generosity are a legacy of its past. Bahrainis are a remarkably urbane people, whether you encounter them at the hotel or restaurant, in a taxi, or if you ask to take a photo of them... they are unlikely to say no.

You can wander around the souqs with the peace of mind that you won't be pestered by vendors touting for business.

Plenty of tourist attractions are free or cost next to nothing, as if the Bahrainis are conscious not to appear too greedy when it comes to sharing their culture.

Visiting the dhow building yard in Muharraq, popular with tourists, we suggested to the owner that he should introduce an entry fee to support this craft at risk of extinction, but the proposal met with distaste: it seemed inconceivable to charge people who are interested in your livelihood and only natural to step away from your tools and workbench for a short while to show people around.

Impossible to refuse an invitation to enjoy a cardamom-infused coffee.

An invitation to have coffee or a bite to eat is an act of pure generosity, one it would be rude to refuse (*see box on next page*).

## Habits and customs

**Purification**

When you get to your hotel, you might be greeted with a bowl of scented water to wash your hands, or even a censer. This type of fumigation is a traditional custom. To absorb the fragrant smoke, in your hair especially, carefully lean over and tilt your head.

**Cardamom coffee**

If you're invited for a cardamom coffee, a ritual in every Gulf country, always hold your cup with your right hand. Putting the cup down on the tray is a signal for more to be poured. If you have had enough of a caffeine fix, gently shake the cup and your host will understand.

**Full to the brim?**

When eating, be it a full meal or a dessert, before tucking in wait until all the dishes have been brought to the table and generously served. It's polite to try everything you're offered out of respect for your hosts. Leave some food on your plate, to show that you've had your fill, but not too much or it suggests the meal wasn't to your liking.



## A passion for Arabian thoroughbreds

The **Bahrain International Trophy**, with its 600,000 dollar first prize, was introduced in 2019, showing just how determined the kingdom is to establish itself as a premier horse-racing destination. This high-ranking international event showcases the quality of Bahraini horses in competition and an ancestral passion for what is regarded as the finest equine breed in the world: the Arabian thoroughbred. Horse-racing season is a popular affair, and the season lasts from November to May, with two races a month more or less. Attending a meeting at the **racecourse in Riffa** is a chance to join the Bahrainis for a moment of pure excitement... all the more surprising when you consider that betting isn't permitted.

The Arabian is a featherweight thoroughbred, measuring between 14 and 15.2 hands and weighing in at no more than 400 kg.

But it's a prince of the desert of rare elegance, recognisable by its refined head and high tail carriage. While its coat is not characteristic, the horse is immediately recognisable thanks to its straight, slightly concave muzzle. Battle-hardened by the region's extreme climate conditions, it's a resilient breed as demonstrated by the Prophet Muhammad during his conquests. Today, it's a champion of **endurance races**, one of the Bahrainis' favourite sporting events, in which Arabian horses are frequently the winners.

The island is home to an estimated 12,000 horses, a staggering number for such a tiny country. More astonishing still are the **royal stables** where they are making every effort to preserve and rear purebred Arabians in Bahrain,

The Arabian horse is recognisable by its straight, slightly concave muzzle.

regarded as among the most beautiful horses in the world. Bahrain being an island, crossbreeding has been controlled, and the breed is one of the purest in the world. Natural selection is the rule and no animal is up for sale: all that matters is the excellence and conservation of this slice of natural heritage. While the royal stables are not open to visitors, you can admire these magnificent beasts by attending the Friday meetings at the racecourse in Riffa.

## Invincible dromedaries

Camel racing is a tradition still alive and kicking in modern-day Bahrain. There are a number of camel farms across the kingdom. The best of the bunch, hooves down, is the **Royal Camel Farm** *(p. 54)*, in Janabiyah, open to the public. This farm has bred many champions to have competed in some of the most prestigious races in the UAE, Qatar and Saudi Arabia.



## Falconry, the sport of kings

Falconry is deeply rooted in Bahrain's culture. This ancient hunting practice was the privilege of the elite and remains a favourite pastime among the country's high society, who consider it an art form. Competitions are held in Bahrain as well as Qatar, the UAE and Saudi Arabia to single out the fastest falcons. This 'sport of kings' has recently become popular with a younger crowd, although the prices are still prohibitive: a bird of prey costs anywhere from 4,000 to 200,000 dollars.

Falconry schools and clubs are nonetheless sprouting up across the kingdom, opening the sport up to the masses through classes and certificates. These facilities also fulfil an environmental role, protecting the falcons which are mostly imported from Europe. When exploring the island's desert regions, it's not uncommon to see a falcon gliding in the air before descending on its prey.

### The white donkeys of Saar

The Bahraini white donkey isn't just a zoological curiosity, it can also be a champion in the races held every Friday, at sundown, in the town of Saar. It's a 'tradition' that dates back barely 40 years but seems as rooted in local culture as a centuries-old oak tree. Drawing an excited crowd, races take place on an improvised track next to a busy main road. People even come from Saudi Arabia or Qatar to see the beautiful white donkeys – some prettified with henna dye – run full pelt in these unbridled events. There's no strict rules or regulations for these competitions, much to the dismay of animal rights groups, but it's a moment of pure joy for the local populus.

# Fusion cuisine

## A smorgasbord of local and global flavours

Historically at the nexus of multiple civilisations and trade routes, Bahrain has an incredibly varied food scene. Traditional Bahraini cuisine is delicious and fragrant. Your taste buds will be tantalised by the flavours of sweet spices, aromatic herbs, floral syrups, dried fruit, grilled fish and delicately spiced local dishes. Iranian, Indian, Arabian and Middle Eastern influences are blended together in a mouthwatering fusion of aromas and colours.

Cuisines from all over the world are well represented across the kingdom, and whatever you're in the mood for, Bahrain has just the place for you. Because of the island's geographic location, it's possible to discover types of cuisine that are unfamiliar to the European palate, such as specialities from central Asia or southern Africa. An unbelievably diverse range of taste sensations awaits inquisitive foodies, from Bahraini classics to far-flung fare.

The Bahraini breakfast served on small plates and made for sharing lets you taste a range of local specialities.

## Female-led cuisine

Open to the world, Bahraini cuisine has evolved apace with its society, combining tradition and modernity. It's a scene on which talented female chefs shine brightly. Independent and highly educated, Bahraini women are seasoned entrepreneurs and more and more restaurants are under the helm of female owners and chefs displaying the technical flare, personality and creativity that are the pride of the island.

## In Baharat kingdom

A trip to Bahrain wouldn't be complete without sampling some of its traditional dishes. The **Bahraini breakfast** is, thankfully, unavoidable. Served on small plates or bowls, it's made for sharing and lets you taste a range of local specialities. Starting with ***balaleet***, sweet vermicelli noodles topped with a plain egg omelette; ***baydh tomat***, scrambled egg with chopped fresh tomato; ***nikhee*** and ***alo,*** chickpeas and sautéed potato croquettes respectively, both cooked in spices; and lastly ***ful***, puréed broad beans. All this is usually served with ***khubz***, a type of flat bread baked in a *tannur*, the traditional clay oven. Arabic coffee – ***gahwa,*** – flavoured with cardamom, or ***karak***, the Middle Eastern equivalent of chai tea served with milk are the beverages served with the *bahrani breakfast*, possible accompanied by ***zinjibari,*** triangle-shaped doughnuts filled with sweet cream or cheese. We heartily recommend going into the city for breakfast: it's a meal popular with Bahrainis and the ideal opportunity to mingle with the locals (*Addresses pp. 70 and 72).*



For other meals, the famous ***Machboos*** is Bahrain's national dish: rice seasoned with fragrant spices served with tender, fall-off-the-bone chicken or lamb, popular all over the Gulf region and wider Middle East. Every country has its own version and in Bahrain one special ingredient sets it apart from the rest: a mix of eight spices and ingredients called ***baharat***, a blend of cardamom, paprika, coriander, nutmeg, clove, cinnamon, black pepper and *lumee*, tangy, sun-dried lemons. An aromatic and delicious dish, don't depart without trying it! Another rice dish popular across the kingdom is ***biryani***, served with meat or prawns and influenced by Indian cuisine. The recipe is enhanced with fried onion, raisins, flaked almonds or pine nuts and local spices, lending it that extra Bahraini touch!

## Food fit for an emperor!

Fish is abundant in Bahrain, and the spectacle of watching boats unload their cargo is sure to tempt you to taste the local catch. The most common fish are ***hamour*** (grouper) – a white, flaky-fleshed fish found in the Gulf's waters – and ***sheri***, or emperor fish. Both are typically served fried or grilled with herbs, lemon and garlic. In some restaurants (*p. 71)*, you get to choose your own fish and seafood and how they are cooked. Prawns are popular too, sautéed in ***ghee*** (clarified butter commonly used in Arabian cooking) and served with rice. You'll often find them on the menu in the form of ***Chebeh Rubyan***, shrimp balls made with herbs and spices then cooked in a tomato, onion and

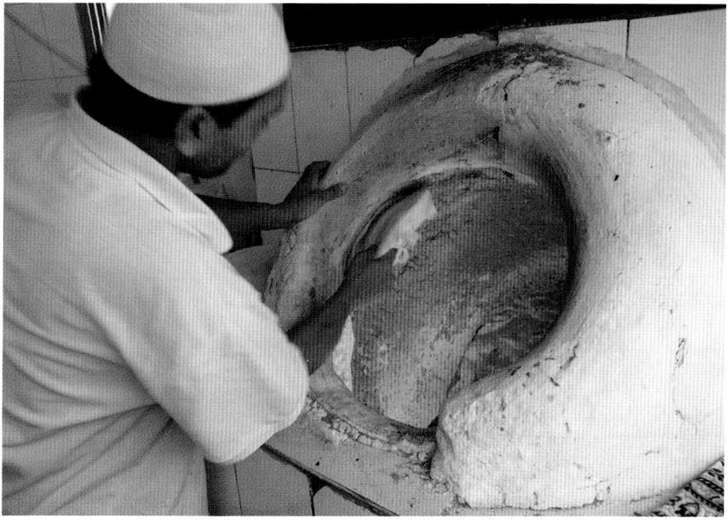

©Eric Sander (ericsander.com)

A baker in Manama Souq making bread in the traditional tannur clay oven.



tamarind paste sauce which brings a delicious citrusy note.

## End on a sweet note...

No true foodie will end a meal before satisfying their sweet tooth. And Bahraini desserts are as generous and calorific as they come! The famed ***halva***, a thick sesame paste, is mixed with rose syrup, saffron, cardamom and dried fruit, served warm or at room temperature. While historically this speciality was imported into the Gulf from Zanzibar via the trade routes with the Sultanate of Oman, Bahraini halva has been produced on the island for over 170 years by the **Showaiter** family, with almost no competition. So little in fact that locals have come to call this treat 'Showaiter halva' (*p. 84*).

Even milder for our Western palates, ***mahalabia*** is a milk pudding flavoured with rose or orange blossom water and a sprinkling of pistachios. ***Muhammar*** is sweet rice mixed with saffron and rose water.

Arabic coffee is a symbol of welcome and hospitality in Bahrain. Served in *dallah*, typical coffee pots with a crescent-shaped spout, and poured into *finjan*, small handle-less cups, it is offered at any time of day, often accompanied by succulent dates grown in the kingdom.

# Tala Bashmi, an icon of Bahrain's new food scene

The first thing you spot when you enter **Fusions by Tala** (*p. 72*) is the glass-walled kitchen, the bustling domain of the chef on show to every diner. Sporting a snug baseball cap and chef's coat and apron, totally absorbed in the preparation of her dishes, Tala Bashmi works with deliberate but delicate gestures. The four chefs in her team busily attend to their tasks behind her. The focused but cheerful quartet seem to spin around the kitchen in a graceful balletic display. It takes just a few minutes of observing Tala to get a sense of what she is about: her aura fills the space. Determined, generous, meticulous... the most celebrated chef in the kingdom is the centre of attention, and not just from where I'm sitting but of restaurateurs the world over.

## From footie to food

Cooking was not in Tala Bashmi's life plan. A high-level athlete, she was a defensive midfielder playing in Bahrain's national women's football team. Proud to represent her country, dedicated, combative, she trained hard, set her sights high and played at international level... until the day she suffered an injury – striking a fatal blow to her promising career. Without looking back, she pivoted towards a couple of her other passions: art and pastry-making, the latter steering her career on a path to becoming a chef. After studying in Switzerland, she returned to Bahrain and in 2014 joined the **Gulf Hotel**, Bahrain's original 5-star hotel. Tala grasped the ins and outs of being a commis chef in a year. After just two more years, her relentless determination and enthusiasm were recognised by the hotel management who promoted her to the position of executive chef, promising Tala her name above the door if she could turn a profit within a year. A challenge this fighter achieved with flying colours.

## One of the top restaurants in the Middle East

Tala Bashmi's cuisine combines Bahraini culinary traditions and international influences with a new level of finesse. She never ceases to excite and enchant foodies from the region and the four corners of the globe. Tala sources her ingredients from local producers and the fish market for her always seasonal menu. Fond of her native island, she showcases the kingdom's heritage, its spices, its flavours, its unique specialities, creating innovative recipes with her boundless imagination. Soon to turn 35 years old, the chef – snubbed in her early days by many of her male peers – has made her mark and inspired a whole new generation. Fusions by Tala is now recognised as one of the best restaurants in the Middle East and North Africa. Tala Bashmi, a big name and radiant presence, putting Bahrain squarely on the foodie map.

A successful career change for Tala Bashmi, a former professional footballer

**Collection managed by Philippe Orain**

| | |
|---|---|
| **Editorial Director** | Éric Boucher |
| **Editorial Secretary** | Émilie Vialettes |
| **Editors** | Serge Bathendier, Victor Dalmas, Nora Gherras, Éric Boucher |
| **Translator** | LanguageWire |
| **Contributors** | Theodor Cepraga, Costina-Ionela Lungu (**Cartography**), Véronique Aissani, Carole Diascorn (**Cover**), Marion Capera, Marie Simonet, Ilona D'Angela (**Picture Editors**), Bogdan Gheorghiu, Cristian Catona, Hervé Dubois, Pascal Grougon (**Prepress**), Dominique Auclair (**Production Manager**)<br>Plans and maps: © MICHELIN 2023 and Cartographic data © The contributors of OpenStreetMap http://www.openstreetmap.org under licence ODbL 1.0 http://opendatacommons.org/licenses/odbl/ |
| **Acknowledgements** | We are very grateful to Hubert Barbier de Chalais who had the idea for this guide. |
| **Graphic design** | Laurent Muller (interior layout)<br>Véronique Aissani (cover) |
| **Advertising Sales and Partnerships** | contact.clients@editions.michelin.com<br>*The content of any advertising pages contained in this guide is the sole responsibility of advertisers.* |
| **Contacts** | Your opinion is essential to improving our products.<br>Help us by answering the questionnaire on our website: editions.michelin.com<br>**Published in 2024** |



Photo credits pp. 4-5
(left to right and top to bottom)

©Eric Sander (ericsander.com)
©Eric Sander (ericsander.com)
Philippe Orain/Michelin
Eric Boucher/Michelin
©Eric Sander (ericsander.com)
Philippe Orain/Michelin
©Eric Sander (ericsander.com)
Nour El Refai

**MICHELIN Éditions**
A French SAS (simplified stock company) with capital of 487,500 EUR
57 rue Gaston Tessier – 75019 Paris (France)
Paris RCS (Trade and Companies Register): No. 882 639 354


Registration of copyright: 03-2024 – ISSN 0293-9436
Typography/Photoengraving: MICHELIN Éditions Paris
Printer: Estimprim, Autechaux
Printed in France: 02-2024

ISO14001 certified facility
Printed on sustainably sourced paper